Ellen Young Patton

Mignonette

Ellen Young Patton

Mignonette

ISBN/EAN: 9783744652407

Printed in Europe, USA, Canada, Australia, Japan

Cover: Foto ©Thomas Meinert / pixelio.de

More available books at **www.hansebooks.com**

MIGNONETTE

Gathered in Hours of Pain: May its

Sweetness Distill for Many

Hearts and Homes,

Is the Wish of

The Author,

ELLEN PATTON.

ATCHISON, KANSAS:

1883

Entered according to Act of Congress, in the year 1883, by Ellen Patton, in the Office of the Librarian of Congress at Washington.

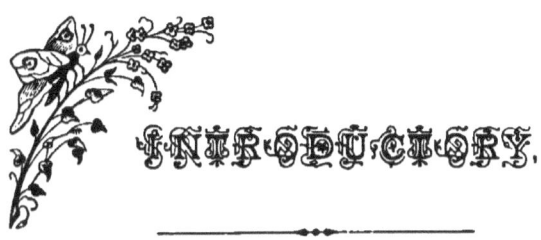

Introductory.

I BRING a sprig of Mignonette,
    With dews of night it still is wet;
Leaves of lemon, buds of rose,
Their jars of fragrance will unclose.

Sometimes we crush the sweetest thing,
For finer perfume that may cling;
Sometimes God breaks the gentlest heart
To make its hidden sweetness start.

The night is sometimes full of stars,
More often crossed by cloudy bars;
But morning comes to every soul,
And Heaven is the Christian's goal.

Accept my bunch of posies, friend,
May they with all life's hardness blend;
With faith and love I tie together
An antidote for stormy weather.

Ho! Pilot! What of the night;
And what of the angry sea?
Can you bring me safe to land?
I have trusted my life to thee.

INDEX

SONGS OF HOPE.

	PAGE.
June's Consolation	9
Among the Grapes	12
My Dove	13
Twilight Reveries	15
Go Work in my Vineyard	17
Song of the Night	20
Empty and Full	22
By the Riverside	24
In Simon's House	26
Lo! I Come; Be Ye also Ready	28
Herbert and Reginald	30
Swing Low	31
Prayer	33
Yielded Up	34
Star Gleams	36
Comfort	38
March of the Ages	40
Ways of Loving Jesus	43
An Afternoon Talk	47
The Ministry of Pain	49
Trusting	50
The Cedar Tree	52
Nature's Prophecies	53
Redemption Draweth Nigh	55
The Gate of Prayer	56
The Sea and the Light-house	59
Grapes of Eschol	61
Touch and Be Healed	62
Slipping Away	64
Wayside Journey	66
A Song	68

INDEX.

Treasures	69
Soaring and Singing	70
Day is Breaking	72
A Lump of Clay	73
Only Leaves	75
Thinking and Acting	77
Foreshadowings	79
Beside the Stream	80
A Song by the Wayside	81

MISCELLANEOUS.

Down in the Trenches	83
Flowers and Women	86
The Midnight Cry	88
Easter Hymn	90
Coming Home	91
A Winter Idyl	93
Peace and Good Will	95
My Lesson	97
Rizpah	98
Crayon Sketches	101
Sleep	103
Little Brown Hen	105
Indian Summer is Dead	107
Love	108
Broken Shackles	109
Warp and Woof	111
The Mother's Lament	112
Hagar	114
The Day and I	117
Belshazzar's Feast	118
A Temperance Dream	120
The Two Brooks	123
The Bridge O'er Which the Babies Go	125
Nest Building	128
Baby's Poem	129
The Twins	131
Thoughts for Scientists	132
Leaves from Gethsemane	134

God's Mercy	136
Maids and Apple Blossoms	138
A Soul at Auction	140
A Woman's Protest	141
Looking Out	143
To One who asked for a Song	145
After Christmas	147
A Little Sermon	149
Woman	150
The Call	151
The Bow in the Cloud	153
Summer Has Come	156
Silver Wedding Song	157
Red Clover	160
Answer to the Nation's Prayer	162
Christ's Transfiguration	164
A Mamma to Keep	166
Jesus and the Woman	167

Childs Department.

Little Boy Blue	169
To Gracie's Picture	171
Christmas Carol	172
Staining of the Leaves	174
Going Fishing	177
Mother Goose Revised	180
The Kitten Story	182
Whisky Punch	183
Going a Maying	185
Nellie's Chatter	187
Red Breast Robin	188
Two Johnnies	189
Snow Flake	190
Somebody's Coming	191
Little Bare Feet	193
Longing for Spring	195
Baby	196
Didn't Want to be an Angel	197
Christmas Bells	199

SONGS OF HOPE.

June's Consolation.

COME gently sailing in, through window opened wide,
    The musky scent of roses white and red;
Methinks the perfumed air will flush my lonely room—
    Pale grief will swoon away; the God o'erhead,
That guides the foam-white clouds upon their way,
Bears me upon his loving breast to-day.

The roses thrilled with life and burst their swaddling
    bands,
    To flaunt their plumes and coquette with the sun;
So, let me cast the half-crushed shell in which I hide,
    For one that's fringed with glory; life is won
By climbing like the vine toward the light;
The sweet, sweet day is ever born of night.

I close my eyes, and silver-footed silence reigns,
    Peace folds her wings, content awhile to bide,
And love drops amber honey on my parching lips;
    How good it is within God's arms to hide.
Just hear the blue-bird burst his throat with praise,
A wreath of song to clasp around my days.

A song, yes, steep my spirit in thy subtle breath,
    And charm away my grief, O bloom and bird,
While I lean back in trust upon my downy rest—
    Sweet promises I find within God's word.
But late there burned within my room a light;
Love lit and fed it—ah! 'twas very bright.

The light burn'd dimmer, dimmer still, and then went out;
    The lute of one sweet voice had broken strings,
'T was not attuned to human harmonies, and now
    I mourn my lute, while sandaled sorrow flings
Her soft, dark mantle o'er my quivering form;
I tremble like the aspen in this storm.

Trill on, O prayerful bird, and royal blossoms, burn,
    My darling loved you both, and he may stay
To heed thy gracious ministry unset to words;
    I think he is not far from me to-day—
I seem to feel him near, e'en as blind eyes
Can feel the light poured out through azure skies.

They built a poem 'round my pureling while he slept—
  The fragrant, dainty blossoms on his breast,
The scarlet spotted ones atween the two white feet—
  How lovely thou didst seem in that deep rest!
But up some emerald steep thy soul did climb,
Where snow-white lilies blow, unknown in time.

I lightly soar with thee up to those beamy plains,
  Where full-banked rivers run, thick fringed with flowers;
And I in turn draw thee, by love's immortal chain,
  To share my earth, and I share heaven's bowers.
Ah! love does not forget, and love is strong,
I'll leap the sea of death ere very long.

Love is the God within us, and will grandly reign
  When all the coarser fiber is burned out;
So, gleaming cohorts, stand upon that wave-worn shore
  With all your dove-like plumage on, and shout—
"Ye gates of purple and of gold, unroll,
To welcome in another storm-beat soul."

Among the Grapes.

I sit upon the hill-side slope, the day is dying slow,
    And all the idle autumn winds are wandering to and fro;
The western sky is glorified with mingled gray and gold,
While night shakes out her shining robes, with odors in each fold,
    And all the while sad whip-poor-will,
    Pipes forth his song beyond the hill.

The song repeated o'er and o'er, it holds a vague unrest,
As if the mystery of grief were trembling in thy breast;
As if the heart of Nature were stirred with some swift pain,
And you uttered it for her in verse, again and once again.
    You make me sad, sweet whip-poor-will,
    Piping your song beyond the hill.

All round about me vine leaves are curling in the breeze,
And purple grapes breathe incense, that floats above the trees;
The chalice of the night-wind is filled with subtle wine;
In this enchanted atmosphere I weave my dreamy rhyme;
    While minor tones of whip-poor-will,
    Make melody beyond the hill.

All the ruby globes around me seem whispering of a time
When all their purple hearts will be exhaled in wine.
Must everything be crushed till it yields its finest sweet?
Must gold lie in the crucible and feel the furnace heat?
    My answer comes from whip-poor-will;
    Who sings his plaintive ditty still.

Grapes, gold and hearts are crushed, or feel the touch of
    fire;
So in the martyr flames I sit, and tune my trembling lyre.
O band of pain that holds me fast, yet leaves me strength
    to sing,
    Up broken stairways of my heart, praise climbs to
        Christ our King.
    I join the flute-voiced whip-poor-will,
    Who chants his anthem o'er the hill.

My Dove.

A LITTLE white dove flew into my breast,
    And pleaded for rest.
I folded the birdling close with my arm,
    And soothed its alarm.

We grew so happy—my white dove and I,
    Joy came from the sky;

Just now I sit here making my moan—
My birdie has flown.

There came a loud call, clear and wond'rous sweet;
I sprang to my feet,
And cried in my pain, "Ah! let the dove stay;
Don't bereave me to day."

It slipped from my hold, I could not detain,
With my passion of pain;
A cup full of gall was pressed to my lip,
And I took but a sip.

It was bitter; I reached it back to the Lord,
And uttered no word;
He spoke; His love made my wounded heart thrill,
"Peace, child, and lie still.

"Lay thy burden on me; I'll drink up the gall,
And bear thee through all;
When the pain is hardest lie on my breast,
Like a bird in its nest.

"I'll take care of the dove, and bear thee along
Till thou hearest its song."
So, step after step, with uplifted eye,
I climb to the sky.

When at last I come to death's sullen shore,
Christ will ferry me o'er;
There I will find, in the land of His love,
My tender white dove.

Twilight Reveries.

I SAT in the door of my cottage,
   At the close of a long summer's day;
Before me were stretches of woodland,
   And the hills in the distance lay;
The shadows were folding around me,
   The many sweet voices of night
Were charming away my sadness,
   And turning my soul to the light.

I thought how oft in the gloaming,
   Our dear Lord had wandered away,
While the twelve, who watched Him and loved Him,
   Were saying, "He goeth to pray."
Oh, garden, surpassing all others,
   Whose dews have been brushed by a God;
Oh, sorrow, that we cannot fathom,
   When Jesus lay prone on the sod.

Thy grasses had bloody baptism,
　　Thy olive trees swayed to His moan,
While he sweat drops of blood in the garden,
　　And prayed there in meekness alone.
And now I sit here in the twilight,
　　Thinking over these sweet thoughts of Thee;
The smile of Thy love, warm and tender,
　　Seems resting a blessing on me.

Thy gentle voice says, "Bear thy burden;
　　Shrink not from the pain and the loss;
I bore, I suffered, I conquered—
　　Heaven lies by the way of the cross.
Look off to the hills of Mount Zion,
　　There lieth thy hope and thy rest;"
And my heart riseth up while it singeth,—
　　I'll trust Him, for He knoweth best.

The crossing of death may be nearer
　　Than I think, as I sit here to-night,
But its waters can never o'erwhelm me,—
　　My faith will be then turned to sight;
I will see my dear Lord standing ready
　　To lead me across by the hand,
And if I grow faint in the Jordan,
　　His arms will bear safely to land.

Go Work in My Vineyard.

'TWAS an early hour in the morning,
   The silvery light of the stars,
Was all blown out from the heavens;
   But up through her eastern bars
The bride of the day was climbing,
   Away from her feet there rolled
Her robes, where mingled the pearl and gray,
   So daintily trimmed with the gold.

While waiting, a cry came stealing,
   Straight down from the rosy sky:
"Child, go work in my garden to-day,
   And go ere the sun rises high."
"O, let me enjoy the morning,
   So dewy, so cool, so fair;
My hands are too soft and white for work,
   Some other must take my share."

So I idled through all the morning,
   Each hour seemed long as a day;
Gathered some flowers, and heard the bird,
   That was singing over the way.

At noon the voice came back to me,
"O, the weeds are growing apace,
I have looked but cannot find a hand
    That is willing to take *your* place."

I thought I would go to the garden,
    And sit in its pleasant shade;
Perhaps would direct the toilers,
    But could not give them my aid,
For now is the heat and the burden,
    Of all the long, weary day;
The sun shines down like a furnace fire,
    Would my unskilled labor pay?

I saw an army of toilers,
    Working away for the King;
The sweat dropped down from weary brows,
    But each had a song to sing;
They loosened the ground around each plant,
    They watered with dews of grace,
And each looked up with a smiling trust,
    Straight into the Master's face.

They gathered the sheaves and bound them,
    They thought of a harvest home;
The day was slipping adown the sky,
    And sweet rest was sure to come.

I looked at a little corner,
  Thick grown with bramble and weed,
The sun and air, they had no chance
  For helping the precious seed.

I looked at my tender hands again,
  And then at the western sky,
Sprang to my feet with a trembling heart,
  Resolved that I would try.
Dear Lord, the day is almost gone,
  But I will labor till night;
My bleeding hands were torn by thorns,
  But at "evening time 'twas light."

My tears rained down, they turned to prayers;
  One stood in the gloaming by,
And cheered me with His loving smile,
  He heard my feeblest cry.
Ah, now I feel how light my task!
  Henceforth my pride shall be,
To keep this garden corner clear,
  Till Jesus calls out for me.

A Song of the Night.

MOUNT ZION, the city that I love—
   Ah, how my weary feet
Are pressing along the narrow way,
   Toward the golden street;
Sweet way-marks of the Lord I find,
   Till my soul, like a lark on the wing,
Flies out of my breast and soars away;
   And this is the song I'll sing:
     "My Lord has risen, and I will rise,
     Straight up to the gates of Paradise."

Sometimes when the purple night comes down,
   And the road-way of the sky
Is lighted up with the starry lamps,
   I long for my home on high.
I look for Jesus—He does not come
   To fold me up close to His breast;
But a strong, swift angel flutters down,
   And whispers, "He'll give you rest."
     So out in the night I send my voice,
     "He loves you still, faint heart rejoice."

The tender gardener loves the plant,
   When he clips each bud and bloom ;
He would train it up to a larger growth—
   For finer blossoms make room.
I, like the silver, must be refined,
   And, when thrust in the hottest fire,
Lift pleading eyes away to the King—
   To His praise will I tune my lyre.
      No bird of the wood will give song so sweet,
      As I will pour out at the Master's feet.

My carrier dove I will speed along,
   Winged by trust and loving prayer;
No gem of the mines would give such joy
   To Him who is bearing my care.
The faint, sweet odors that hide in the east,
   They brought unto Mary's blest child.
The broken spirit, the service of love,
   I offer the Lamb undefiled.
      He hung on the cross. Ah, rapture ; ah, pain !
      He died on the cross, but He liveth again.

Sweet lilies that rock on Galilee's sea—
   Soft winds that have over them blown—
With your spicy breath fly away, away,
   To Him who sits on the throne.

Break into praise, O mountain and vale—
   Cold heart, be enkindled to flame;
Waves of the ocean and crash of the gale,
   Chant praises to His precious name.
     Immanuel triumphs, his flag is unfurled.
     The babe of the manger has conquered the world.

Empty and Full.

THERE are empty chairs all over the land;
   I've an empty heart and an empty hand
     For the Lord of Glory to fill;
But alas! what will fill the little chair,
And how shall I wreathe the cross I bear,
     Or yield to the Savior, my will.

Our dear laddie's memory fills the chair,
   The blue, blue eyes and the gold brown hair,
  The rose red mouth, so pure, so sweet;
In fancy gleams out that high, white brow,
Through a mist of tears I see thee now,
   From thy dimpled hands to thy feet.

Around the cross I'll lovingly twine,
An evergreen rare, not culled in time—
    Where death never comes it grew;
The fragrant white blossoms of perfect love,
Trail over and down from the land above;
    They are gemmed with heavenly dew.

Thus I deck my cross, and my will I lay
At the Father's feet, and humbly pray,
    May my will be made thine own;
Oh, heaven will not be empty to me,
My mother and two sweet sons I'll see,
    When I bow by the great white throne.

Yes, heaven is full of little white souls,
The tide of their lives it rolls and rolls,
    But to break at the dear Lord's feet.
Oh, empty me of my passion and pain,
To fill me up with the Christ again;
    Make thy purpose in me complete.

By the River Side.

I CAME to the shore of a wide, turbid river,
  The waves they were hungry and rose to the land;
The soul that was in me shrank back with a shiver,
  Appalled at the sight of the ruin decked strand.
    But over the tide fairest flowers were blowing,
    And over the waters I fain would be going.

While I wait, the night time is silently falling,
  And only one star breaks the black of the sky;
While over the river sweet voices are calling,
  "Fear not to launch out, though the billows run high;
    For here are your loved ones, and here is the glory
    You have read of so oft in the old, old story."

Yes, friend after friend has gone out through this portal,
  The mate of my spring-time, the babe of my breast;
And now over yonder they stand up immortal,
  While I still linger here, though longing for rest.
    But ah, this deep river, this terrible river,
    Ho! boatman, come quickly and bear me swift
      thither.

The sheaves that I gathered, Oh ! fain would I carry,
  To the Lord of the temple that, gleaming, you see ;
The night shutteth down, why so long do you tarry ?
  Come, take o'er my treasures, and with them take me.
    The winds bear unto me sweet odors of heaven,
    The song of the blest to my earth ears is given.

At last beareth out from the harbor eternal,
  A white boat with sails of a silvery hue ;
I soon will be walking in fields ever vernal,
  Where the sun never sets, with the skies ever blue.
    Yes, over the river, the wild, cruel river,
    I'm going to live with my darlings forever.

In the prow there is one with an eye like the morning,
  With brow that's majestic, the grace of a king;
The sunlight of glory his pathway adorning,
  As the bark speedeth o'er like a bird on the wing.
    I no more am a pilgrim of labor and sorrow,
    But glide out from time to eternity's morrow.

Farewell to you, friends, who press down to the river,.
  To earth my ear dulls and my eyes they grow dim ;
I am entering now on the golden forever,
  My spirit is tuned to a grand triumph hymn.
    How sweet is the rhyme of the waters smooth flowing,
    They wait for me yonder—good bye—I am going.

In Simon's House.

THE haughty Pharisee had asked
    The lowly Nazarene to dine;
A woman from the city came,
    While they upon the couch recline.
Behind the Lord she stood and wept;
    She bathed with tears those weary feet,
And dried them with her ebon hair—
    Ah, love and homage, sweet, most sweet.

Those kisses were unspoken prayer,
    And when the alabaster vase
Had spilt its sweetness on the air,
    The loving Lord gave grace for grace.
The haughty Simon thought with pride
    Were he a prophet, Christ would know
This is a sinner—He would chide
    Her sin and weakness—bid her go.

The woman wept, and Jesus knew
    The thought that lurked in Simon's heart;
This is the picture that He drew,
    And held it up with guileless art:

"There were two debtors owed one king,
  One sum was large, the other small;
Nothing they had, and naught could bring,
  So freely he forgave them all."

"Now which would love the most, think you?"
  "The one that had the most forgiven."
"You are right; 'tis not the favored few
  That find the royal road to heaven.
This woman came with gentle tread,—
  You gave no water for my feet,
No kiss, no ointment for my head;
  But she hath given service meet."

"Yes, she hath lavished love and tears,
  Kisses and ointment, and her hair
Hath wiped my feet; the guilt of years
  I wipe from off her soul; 'tis rare
To find such trusting love below.
  Then go in peace, have faith in me."
So forth she went, white as the snow,
  Her debt was canceled, she was free.

"Lo! I Come: Be Ye Also Ready."

WHILE my soul sat aloof from all wildering care,
   A vision of glory and grandeur swept o'er me;
I lapsed into dreaming so rich and so rare,
   That my griefs slipped away—angel wings soft upbore me.
Sweet Jesus, the theme of my fancies so glowing,
   As the babe sweetly smiling, as the man shedding tears,
While they wailed o'er the dead, life and love was bestowing,
   He was stilling the tempest and calming men's fears.

He was bearing the cross, and by rude hands uplifted
   Was nailed to the wood, with the thorns on his brow;
Oh, passion divine! the sweet fragrance hath drifted
   From thy living and dying—it thrilleth me now.
He was laid in the tomb—lo! He burst from its holding;
   Joy, joy, He hath triumphed! Christ is raised from the dead;
Ascending to heaven, the swift clouds enfolding
   The glorified form that had suffered and bled.

This is the sweet message He left at His going,
   "As I go, will I come—dear children, believe me;"
The waves of the melody round me are flowing,
   Jesus died—Jesus lives—He will never deceive me.

Methinks his descending draws nearer and nearer;
    I am ready—the torch of my soul is aflame;
Earth fadeth, and heaven seems nearer and clearer;
    I will mount to the skies through faith in His name.

Will He come in the morn when the soft breezes stirring,
    The leaves of the trees will they break into praise?
When the sun in clear azure depths is ashining,
    And dewdrops on the grass flash a smile in his rays?
When the flowers are abloom and all nature rejoices,
    The bird notes atremble to burden the air;
Will the strong earth awaken in myriad voices,
    To welcome the Lord who has borne all our care?

Will he come when the moon serenely is shining,
    When the star lamps are gemming the blue of the sky?
While sleep and sweet dreams are man's passions refining,
    Will we wake from our slumbers to meet Christ on high?
If He come in the morning, or come in the night
    When the earth is aglow, and pulsing with beauty;
If tempests and clouds are abroad in their might,
    Calm and firm let us stand at the post of our duty.

No language can utter the glory of heaven,
    No prophet tell over the joy of God's own;

For the ear hath not heard, to the eye is not given,
  The unknown delights of the King on His throne.
Methinks even now heaven's arches are ringing,
  With songs of the ransomed in robes of pure white.
I long to be glorified, long to be singing
  In the land where my God is the joy and the light.

Herbert--Reginald.

BILLOWS of grief go over my soul,
  I'm down in a terrible flood;
Jesus is here the waves to control—
  His agony drew sweat of blood.

My tender babies He bears on His breast,
  And there let me lay down my head;
In a little while He will give me rest,
  And this is the way I am led.

Up a thorn-sprinkled steep I must go,
  Some white blooms are gemming the road,
Friends are grieving for me here below,
  But I go beyond to my God.

He will give me my children again,
  More lovely than ever before;
Will empty my cup of every pain,
  When I land on the heavenly shore.

Swing Low.

THE chariot wheels are rolling,
   The King will come this way:
Wake up, you sleepy virgins,
   He bade you watch and pray.
      Swing low, swing low,
         O shining chariot, swing;
      Our hearts have grown so weary,
         While waiting for our King.

What, sleeping still, and he draws near!
   Your lamps are burning low;
O rouse, and quickly trim the lights,
   The heavens begin to glow.
      . Swing low, swing low,
         O shining chariot, swing;
      Our hearts have grown so weary,
         While waiting for our King.

The sleeping virgins will not wake,
   Their lamps have quite gone out;
Perhaps they hope to buy some oil,
   After the angels shout.
      Swing low, swing low,
         O shining chariot, swing;
      For Sharon's rose is blooming still—
         My soul has cause to sing.

The cloudy door-ways of the sky
   Stand open for the King;
And ranks of angels drift along,
   Like birds upon the wing.
     Swing low, swing low,
       O shining chariot, swing;
     Our hearts have grown so weary,
       While waiting for our King.

The glory of thy golden hair,
   Is floating on the breeze;
The triumph-car drops lower still—
   I fall upon my knees.
     Swing low, swing low,
       O shining chariot, swing;
     Drop down until you touch the earth,
       And lift me to the King.

Thy crown is thorn marks on the brow,
   There's nail marks in each palm;
Lo! all the earth should waken up,
   To chant some holy psalm.
     Swing low, swing low,
       O shining chariot swing;
     I break the bands that hold me down,
       And rise to meet the King.

Prayer.

THE anchor of my soul is prayer,
    The cable line is faith;
It binds me to God's throne, and there
    I'll anchor too in death.

My ship may toss upon life's sea
    Of sorrow and despair—
But, Father, I can come to Thee,
    And calm all storms by prayer.

The perfume Jesus loves is prayer,
    Distilled through tears and pain;
"Commit unto Me all thy care,
    And sing a glad refrain."

Prayer helps the weakest saint to live,
    And bears the dying up;
A glory to each day will give,
    And sweeten every cup.

Prayer armed a Luther for the fray,
    And nerved the Wesley's heart;
Prayer will convert the world to-day,
    If Christians do their part.

The power of prayer is used to-day,
  To quench the fires of hell;
God bless the women as they pray—
  God cause their work to tell.

But men must rouse them for the right,
  And hurl the devil down;
A giant wrong goes out by might—
  Grand deeds will win the crown.

Yielded Up.

MY Jesus He gave me treasures,
  So beautiful, rich and rare,
I had no place to keep them safe,
  So I gave them back to his care.
He laid a white babe upon my breast,
  With eyes so tenderly blue;
My baby fell asleep one day,
  In those loving arms I laid him away.
  And there he is taking his rest.

He gave me a precious mother,
  But I never knew her worth
Till she went away, one autumn day,
  Away from the sorrows of earth.

There came a message so pure, so sweet,
    That the Lord sent down to me:
"I conquered death and will come again;
Your babe and mother will be in my train—"
    I fell in a trance at His feet.

I reknit the links of my life,
    And thought the tide would turn;
My days were set to a minor tune
    I was ever striving to learn.
One treasure, still hid within my heart,
    I guarded it day and night,
Thinking the Lord would let me hold
This lammie, astray from the upper fold—
    Of my life it became a part.

One wet spring day it found a path
    That would take it home again;
I could not woo it back to me,
    But I hold to a golden chain,
And follow along in the upward track,
    In search of the tender thing;
The Lord He heard my plaintive cry,
   Without my lammie, O let me die!
I am sure He will give him back.

One other treasure is left to me—
    I pray the heavenly King,
That into the storehouse of His love,
    This treasure of mine He'll bring.
The jewel of my life I hold,
    And polish it day by day
To make it bright, and pure, and sweet,
Fit to lay down at the Master's feet,
    When I climb to the upper fold.

Star-Gleams.

BEFORE the candles were lighted,
    I sat in a musing mood;
I thought of hopes that were blighted,
    I thought that the Lord was good—
Yes, good when He took my treasure,
    Away from my arms and love;
This life is not all for pleasure,
    But a school for the life above.

Though the task be hard that's given,
   Still I must patiently learn
At the feet of the Master in heaven,
   Till he gives the key to turn
My toil into joy and singing,
   My cross to a shining crown;
The swift hours ever are bringing
   A glory and blessing down.

So let my cup be uplifted
   To catch the gift from above;
From their moorings lives have drifted,
   Forgetting that God is love.
Drifted past peace and the morning,
   Into deep gloom and the night;
They saw not the star's bright dawning,
   Just over yon mountain height.

Lighting the path of the weary,
   Clear shining for all the lost;
With it life cannot be dreary,
   But, ah, the marvelous cost
That set this beacon to blazing!
   Blushing heavens and trembling earth,
A chorus of joy were raising,
   When Bethlehem's Star had birth.

Its light has never grown dimmer,
    Through the lapse of stormy years;
Even now I catch its glimmer,
    Through the mist of falling tears.
It will gild the grave with glory,
    Rob death of his fatal sting,
Shine on when saints tell their story,
    Of triumph through Christ the King.

Comfort.

I WANT to go to the mothers
    Who softly weep,
Because their precious babies
    Have gone to sleep—
Asleep in the Savior's arms,
    And still we cry,
Wringing our hands in agony,
    That they must die.

The cheeks that were lately rosy,
    Have grown so white,
The eyes that were full of sunshine,
    Are filled with night;

The breath that kissed our bosoms
    Has sunk to rest ;
We miss the dainty heads that lay
    Upon our breast.

Let me come into your sorrow,
    And hold your hand ;
We mothers can weep together,
    Over the land.
Let us look off in the distance,
    And we may see
The tiny boats of our darlings,
    Upon the sea.

Whose crystal waves are flowing
    Hard by the throne ;
If we find the children happy
    'T will still our moan.
Dost think we would lose our babies
    When grown to men ?
Dost think the Lord would make a gift
    And take it again ?

O, what would our heaven be
    With babes shut out ?
I think we would surely miss
    The childrens' shout.

If full grown men alone went in
    To heaven's gate,
We all might feel some sorrow,
    When 't was too late.

Dear mothers, can you see the light
    Through all these tears?
The Father gathers joy for us
    In ceaseless years.
The Savior took our darlings
    To draw us home,
And they are simply waiting
    Until we come.

March of the Ages.

I AM sitting apart, and my soul is entranced
    With a vision of splendor and glory;
All the ages of God since time was begun
    Are gathering to tell the old story;
Yes, marshal the years with their fruitage of tears,
    And list to the tales they are telling;
They are marching along so weary and gray,
    While the pibroch of triumph is swelling.

Aye, tell us of Eden and man ere the fall,
　In a voice like the breath of the morning,
When Adam stood up with a soul like the snow,
　And God's smile was his pathway adorning.
Tell us of Noah and the ark that he built,
　How the waves of the deluge 'twas riding;
Tho' the waters covered the face of the earth,
　The spirit of God was still guiding.

Tell how they built on the plains of the east,
　A message in stone for the ages;
The prophets in flesh have crumbled to dust—
　Not so with those rock-written pages;
Backward we read to the springing of time,
　And forward to Jesus appearing:
Praise the Lord, O my soul, cry aloud in thy joy!
　Trim your lamps, for the bridegroom is nearing.

The years sweep along, and they bring into line
　The Law and old Sinai's mountain;
The race presses on in the upward way—
　Again shall we drink from life's fountain.
Hoary years press along, and tell of the time.
　When angels their chorus were singing
"Unto you there is born a Savior this day;"
　The heavens and glad earth were ringing.

In Bethlehem's stable our Jesus was born,
   On Calvary's cross He hung dying;
The grieved earth was clad in darkness that day,
   And strong was the voice of her crying.
He sprang from the grave like a lark from her nest,
   But left us this word at his going:
"I ascend to the Father, again will I come,"
   My peace like a river is flowing.

Then soul, sit apart from the burden of life,
   But hands, be thou strong for each duty;
Watch and wait, like a sentinel at his post,
   For the King will come down in His beauty.
He will come and bring us our darlings again—
   Our treasures from over the river;
We'll catch the sweet chime of the heavenly rhyme,
   And enter our golden forever.

Yes, we shall arise to meet Christ in the skies,
   So life, plume thy wing for the flying;
Up, up, past the pain and the tears of this life,
   Past sin and the torment of dying.
A cloud once caught Him away from the sight
   Of those gazing up into heaven;
Look abroad, O men, read the signs of the times—
   Christ Jesus to you shall be given.

The years have gone by in a stately line,
   Each one has told over its story;
The present swings open a royal gate,
   And there streams through a bright flood of glory.
I sit here and wait, with a smiling trust,
   And feel not the sting of my sorrow;
Strong arms are beneath, and they bear me up,
   Then Jesus may come back to-morrow.

Ways of Loving Jesus.

YOU love the Lord, my little friend?
   Pray tell me how.
"By going on His holy day,
To hear the people sing and pray;
Oh, I can close my eyes, and seem
Wrapped in some bright elysian dream
Of sculptured aisles and cloisters dim,
Where angels chant their praise to Him;
Where incense floats upon the air,
From golden censers saints will bear.
Yes, could I always feel like this,
I'd ask no more for earthly bliss.

When I go home to real life,
Then comes the turmoil and the strife;
My ecstacy is cold and dead,
The spirit's peace and joy have fled."

   Religious poetry you read—
   Dear child, 't will never fit your need;
   The battle's front, heroic strife,
   Will energize and fill your life.
   Dreamers must waken, do and bear,
   If they the crown of life would wear.

My stalwart brother, how do you
Serve Christ, whose love is strong and true?
"I make a prayer whene'er they ask,
Though oft it proves a heavy task.
I have but little grace of speech—
Others can edify and teach;
I help to pay the preacher's due,
The Sunday school I aid some, too,
And ask a blessing of the Lord,
As we draw 'round the well spread board.
Then, mother and the little ones,
Ere daily labor is begun;
Sit down, and I a chapter read,
That seems best suited to our need.

Does not this prove my trust in Him
Who died to ransom us from sin?"

 What handmaids feed the altar's fire—
 Duty or Love, Faith or Desire?
 Art patient when things all go ill?
 Canst sacrifice both wish and will?
 "For love of Me take up the cross,
 And you shall never suffer loss,"
 Said Christ. Brother, this is the test—
 If we can stand it, each knows best.

Sinner, wouldst thou have speech with me?
I am truly glad to welcome thee.
"I *think* I love Him you call Lord,
But don't obey His written word;
His claims press home, I slight His grace,
And turn from the beseeching face.
The world bewilders; sin and strife
Unfit me for a holy life;
And so I'm drifting, drifting still,
The victim of my own free will."
Christ was the victim; He can cure
This lack of love, and make you pure;
The way of truth you plainly know
But in that way you will not go.

Dear calm eyed saint, *you* love the Lord,
I know, before you speak a word.
" I love Him for His love of me,
I love Him, for He makes me free.
Faith's wine invigorates my soul,
The balm of charity makes whole
Life's ills. I let it freely flow
O'er weaknesses of friend or foe.

The mantle patience wove I wear,
And lean upon the staff of prayer;
My zeal is fed by fires that glow
Through summer's heat and winter's snow;
My hair is bleached, my eyes are dim
With years and grief, still I trust Him
Who never will His child forsake,
Though hell should strive my faith to shake.
I ll triumph in a few days more,
And stand upon the other shore ;
I feel the glory shining through,
And soon shall see all things made new.

An Afternoon Talk.

MY daughter, come sit beside me,
    In this golden afternoon ;
I want to talk of the risen Lord—
    Perchance He is coming soon.
I'm in the afternoon of life,
    My sun slips down the sky ;
Only a little while, my dear,
    Will our hands in each other's lie.

Don't cry, my child—that wrings my heart ;
    You see, when our work is done,
We roll it up with a glad content,
    And sit in the light of the sun.
Ah, when I come to the rolling tide,
    The Lord will hold my hand,
Ere I'm aware I'll tread the shore
    Of my Immanuel's land.

I think if Christ came down with a shout,
    From its leash my soul would spring ;
Now I lie like a fettered bird,
    Yet longing to plume my wing.
If He does not come, I'll go to Him—

I cannot much longer stay;
This poor, worn frame is too small a cage—
From its hold let me break away.

I have been climbing all my life,
  But only of late I stand
On Beulah's hills,.where one can see
  Right into the Father's land.
So many have gone to the other side,
  So few are left me here;
Oh, how I long for the harbor of rest—
  Would you hinder my journey, dear?

I lift the anchor and spread my sail,
  I trust and.let go my hold;
And float away to an unknown vale,
  Where one never grows tired or old.
Watch my bark and see it speed,
  Out of the reach of your eye;
You are my child, but I am God's—
  Good bye, my darling, good bye.

The Ministry of Pain.

I WAS so very tired and wanted Rest,
I longed to lay my head upon her breast,
So, softly called for her, she did not come,
And then I cried for Peace, but she was dumb.

Yet one came in and sat close by my side;
"I do not want you here," I wildly cried,
" I have enough to bear, and you are Pain;
You will increase the heat in my poor brain."

She touched my burning brow, and said, " Poor child,
God sent me here to sit a little while;
Now close your weary eyes and hear my song,
I may not tarry here so very long."

I did her bidding; ah, you should have heard,
The music that she made was like a bird;
She sang about the Lord; He moaned and cried—
Pain was the angel then, close by his side.

She sung about the throng that had gone up,
And every one of these drank from Pain's cup,
They deeply drank, but then they left the night,
Their whitened souls escaped into the light.

The song was over and I was alone,
I cannot tell you where sweet Pain had flown;
No, not alone, the Christ looked in my eyes,
And said, "I come for you my child, arise."

"Ah, Master, let me stay, for I would tell,
Pain is thy servant sent, she doeth all things well."
"Then you may stay awhile, there's work to do,
Be ready when I come again for you."

Trusting.

OVER head the sky is gray,
    Underneath God lights the way;
He shows my feet the path to tread—
What care I, with God o'erhead!

Underneath the gloom and storm
Hides a strong and loving arm;
Trusting in that love I go,
Fearing nothing here below.

If he sends me pain, 't is best—
After anguish cometh rest;
Should He give me songs to sing,
Still I hide beneath His wing.

SONGS OF HOPE.

The sun shines on, although we
Half the sunbeams do not see;
Before the sun is in the sky
Songs of birds ascend on high.

Before the snow has left the earth
Flowers are stirring for their birth;
If the small, brown seed can hold
Prisoned in its tiny fold

Germs of life and beauty rare,
Know that in ourselves we bear
A germ that at God's word can spring
Into wondrous blossoming.

I bide my time and patient wait,
Lying low before God's gate;
When it opens, I shall be
Changed for all eternity.

Off will drop my grief and care—
Shining garments I shall wear;
Waiting on, I'll sing my song,
For the waiting won't be long.

The Cedar Tree.

THERE stands by my gate a cedar tree,
    Spicy and green the whole year through;
Now it is preaching a sermon to me,
    As I sit out here in the dark and the dew.
The summer lies dead upon the hill,
    But the cedar tree so thick and so tall,
Is reaching her green arms upward still,
    In spite of the biting frost of the fall.

The cricket is chirping his slumber song,
    The babes have said over their prayers,
And I shall be dreaming ere very long,
    Released from my toils and my cares.
But the cedar tree the whole night through,
    Will be waking and watching the sky;
Be breathing her balm and catching the dew.
    God sendeth to her from on high.

His children should be like my cedar tree,
    Ever fragrant and evergreen too;
This is the message given to me,
    And now I repeat it to you:

Reach up your arms although it be night,
 The blessings are falling like dew,
Though the storm be abroad in all of its might,
 God is able to carry you through.

Nature's Prophecies.

AGAIN I sit in my cottage door—
 The night's soft footstep is on my floor—
Her dusky mantle sweeps to my feet,
The touch of her hand is cool and sweet;
She is proudly decked with moon and star,
That flash from silvery heights afar.

Prophets so sweet of the coming day,
My thoughts uprise and they soar away;
I sit in your light and build my dream,
While angels sing across the stream.
Ah, golden the strands with which I weave!
Golden the hopes to those who believe.

What prophecy rare will nature send,
To teach us of the glorious end?
A cloud once caught the Lord from our sight—
"He cometh with clouds," to end our night.
Sweet Jesus, lift me up to thy breast,
The spirit within me faints for rest.

I never look to a white cloud drift
But fancy whispers; the vail may lift,
And Jesus look down with love lit eyes,
Drawing me up to Him in the skies;
To meet the Lord I will plume my wing—
'T is a sweeter hope than angels sing.

He will come again to set us free—
The Savior they nailed upon the tree;
The poor pierced side, and the blood-stained feet—
I kiss the wounds, it is homage meet.
"He cometh with clouds." "Oh, Lord, how long?"
Let this be the burden of my song.

Mine is the simple trust of a child,
You may say my thought is dim and wild,
That deeper meanings I hide and mar;
I sit by rush light—you by a star.
No matter, it has the same sweet end,
For Jesus *will* come, the sinner's friend

Redemption Draweth Nigh.

A WONDERFUL vision was given to me—
   It came on the wings of the morning;
The stars had withdrawn, and the first rosy flush
   The sky in the east was adorning.
     A voice of silver sweetness
       Comes to me from on high :
     "Look up, you saints of Jesus,
       Redemption draweth nigh."

This glorious message, and virgins asleep!
   Wake up! for the bridegroom is nearing;
Trim your lamps, gird your robes, be ready to greet
   Our Lord, if ye love his appearing.
     The herald still keeps sounding,
       Oh, heed the tender cry :
     "Look up, ye saints of Jesus,
       Redemption draweth nigh."

Is the bride made ready in garments of white?
   Does she know her Husband draws nearer?
That virgins are out with lamps burning bright,
   And the voice of the herald sounds clearer?

Oh, hark! I hear the trumpet blow,
   Swing back the gate on high;
"Look up, ye saints of Jesus,
   Redemption draweth nigh."

The marriage supper is already spread
   For the guests who are joyfully singing;
This feast of the Lord where the wine shineth red—
   'Tis no wonder high heaven is ringing.
   Put on your robes of whiteness,
      For brighter grows the sky;
   "Look up, ye saints of Jesus,
      Redemption draweth nigh."

The Gate of Prayer.

THE hand of a babe may swing it,
   But all of the mighty throes
Of the mighty Father above us,
   Cannot the gateway close.
The weakest soul may shut it,
   Made strong by its unbelief,
Open it flies when touched by the hand
   Of the penitent, dying thief.

My Jesus He gave a promise—
  I came to the gate of prayer;
With trembling touch upon the latch,
  I plead my promise there.
"Whatever thou wilt," He told me,
  I am pleading in His name—
The bolts fly back as though just touched
  By a tongue of heavenly flame.

According unto Thy will I call,
  Believing Thou wilt not deny;
Thou, who hearest the wild bird's note,
  Will list to my trusting cry.
So I am patiently waiting,
  Till the gateway will unroll,
The Father my answer will hand out
  The gift of a human soul.

The soul I will reach back again,
  Into the hands of the Lord,
For surely I can trust the One
  Who never can break His word.
E'en while at the threshold I'm kneeling,
  There trembles along the air,
"To him who loves and keeps my law,
  I will give the answer of prayer."

Up to the gateway is crowding,
   The babe with its curls of gold,
The white-haired man who is traveling on
   With the Lamb to the upper fold;
The mother who mourns with Rachel,
   The man that is weary of sin—
Crowding, crowding, by day and night—
   Can all of these prayers get in?

Can the merciful, patient Father
   Pick out my agonized plea?
So many are pressing, pressing along,
   I wonder will He see me?
The child lisps its "Now I lay me,"
   With never a question or doubt;
If I bow with a child like spirit,
   My cry He will never shut out.

The invalid in her chamber,
   Cries over and over again,
"Jesus who hung on Calvary's tree,
   Give me relief from this pain."
And if the pain is slow to go,
   The peace of the Lord comes down;
The heavy cross of suffering
   Is changed to a golden crown.

Think you the ear of the Lord grows dull,
    That the pitiful heart can't feel
For the lowliest of His children,
    Who there by the gateway kneel?
Rejoice and pray without ceasing,
    The hour of your triumph will come;
My Father loveth the trusting heart,
    And pities the lips that are dumb.

The Sea and the Lighthouse.

THIS life is a troubled ocean, dear,
    There is always an under swell
That whispers of storm and commotion, dear,
    But we yield to its magical spell,
And drift away on a summer sea—
    Go out on a sun flecked tide;
We plan to come back at evening time
    To the shore—but the ocean is wide.

We list to the siren's wooing song,
    And we drift and drift away,
And we never come back to that olden shore
    We left, on that blue summer day.

Our shore is baby's cradle, dear,
　　The other eternity's rim,
And our life has only begun, my dear,
　　When we anchor the boat with Him

Who holdeth the foaming sea in His hand,
　　And watcheth the infant's sleep;
So I sing and trust while floating along,
　　"I am one of the dear Lord's sheep."
There are sunken rocks and breakers ahead,
　　I list to their sullen roar,
And lift my eyes to the gleaming light,
　　That stands on the other shore.

Mariners plowing life's foaming sea,
　　On the highest point of bliss
The lighthouse stands; steer straight ahead,
　　The harbor you cannot miss.
Some shining wave will bear you in,
　　When the even tide has come,
And on the shore our friends will wait,
　　To welcome us safely home.

Grapes of Eschol.

AT the borders of the Promised Land,
Where Jordon spreads her shining sand,
They camped along the river side,
And saw beyond the river's tide
The grapes of Eschol hanging fair;
But even then they did not dare
To enter in and boldly eat.

They sent the spies across to bring
The purple globes that climb and cling
Upon Judea's sunny hills,
And all their musky fragrance spills
As incense on the sun-steeped air;
They longed to taste, but did not dare,
To cross the Jordan with their feet.

Not faith enough to keep the track,
And so the dear Lord turned them back;
Eschol's sweet grapes they could not win,
Because they feared to enter in.
How oft we stand and look across
To Paradise and count the cost,
And to the desert turn again.

And yet how often we might eat
The fruits of "Buelah Land," so sweet;
The spies bring back the clusters rare,
They gather in our nights of prayer;
Come let us linger on the shore,
Until we cross the River o'er,
And lose each earthly stain.

O, Eschol's grapes, I press thy wine,
Till all these border-lands of mine
Grow sweeter, fairer, as I drink;
My feet but linger on the brink
Of Jordan's bank; I soon will go
Beyond the River's narrow flow,
To Heaven's emerald plain.

Touch and be Healed.

I WAS searching my thoughts one idle day,
   For something to braid together,
That would help the storm-tossed souls to bear
   The stress of life's cloudy weather;
For the winds will roar, and the rains will pour,
   The skies are not always smiling;
Come sit by my lamp, the curtain is down,
   And love the long hours is beguiling.

How precious is life when God shuts us in,
  His smile transfigures our sorrow;
We lie on his breast contented to-day,
  And his blessing awaits us to-morrow.
Sometimes we think it has come to an end—
  'We have no more strength for the climbing,
Strong arms are beneath and they lift us up,
  The rounds of God's ladder are shining.

One day the Lord was entreated to come,
  Where a dear little girl was lying;
This was the father's pitiful plea,
  "Come and heal, my daughter is dying."
Lo! as he went on his mission of love,
  The crowd all around him thronging,
A woman came up in the press behind,
  Unspoken her hope and her longing.

She touched but the hem of His garment in faith,
  When virtue went out for her healing;
Trembling she came, confessing her act—
  In fancy I now see her kneeling;
And seeing, I call to the worldweary, come,
  Touch the hem of his garment in gladness;
Bowed down to the earth—he will lift you up,
  Sick at heart—he will cure your sadness.

I would rather go in the strength of the Lord—
  Thus reaching my rest in the mountain—
Would rather be fed by a raven to-day,
  Than drink from earth's sweetest fountain,
If else I would miss the wonderful touch,
  Of healing forever and ever.
Light all afflictions will seem in our eyes,
  When we have crossed over the river.

Slipping Away.

SLIPPING away, the singers and saints,
  Through the beautiful gates of pearl,
And still we sit on the shady side,
And watch them go out on the shining tide
That bears them to the Savior's side,
  Far away from time's mad whirl.

Slipping away, like the scarlet leaf
  Thrown down on the river's breast,
The weaver's thread has found its place,
The arrow has hit its mark with grace,
A smile illumines the dear Lord's face,
  For his saints have entered their rest.

SONGS OF HOPE.

Slipping away to the bright beyond,
   As the song of the birds goes by;
Their lives still freight this lower air,
They have lightly dropped their robes of care,
And climbed away by a golden stair,
   Beyond the amethyst sky.

Stars never set in God's wide sky,
   But burn eternally bright.
Aye, we may weep, but angels sing
Till heaven's highest vault will ring,
And saints fly home with buoyant wing,
   Where their faith is turned to sight.

Slipping away as the years go by,
   Into the white forever;
But all of their work has not been done,
And all of their songs have not been sung,
They could not be by human tongue—
   We will hear them over the river.

Wayside Journey.

I WAS traveling on the wayside,
    Under a broiling sun,
Wishing my task was ended,
    Wishing my journey done;
Yes, long and lonely and weary,
    My way through the burning sand—
Was there no other path that led
    Into the Father's land?

I overtook a winsome babe,
    Its eyes like heaven's blue,
A smile about the rosy mouth;
    Before I hardly knew
I bent to kiss the little one,
    For Jesus was a child;
My wish was changed: Oh, let me be
    Like Christ, the undefiled.

A little farther on I came
    To one so faint and weak
That, as I bent above his form,
    He had no power to speak.

I gave him from my ltttle store,
   And wiped his damp'ning brow,
But even as I strove he died—
   No pain could touch him now.

His passing soul had op'd a gate,
   And left it half ajar;
A glory shone upon my way
   From Bethlehem's lonely star.
So I journeyed along the wayside,
   Finding the sick and sad,
Always I found a word in my heart
   To make the mourner glad.

It was the gentle Lord Himself,
   In every new disguise;
I grew so glad this was the path
   That led up to the skies.
Before I was aware, I came
   Unto my journey's end,
And there He stood to welcome me,
   My Savior and my Friend.

He swung the gate and let me in
   To perfect peace and rest,
And now I sing with joyful heart —
   The Lord He knoweth best.

He guided o'er the toilsome way,
  He counted every tear;
I'm safe at home, yes, safe at home,
  And free from pain or fear.

A Song.

I WILL flee, a wounded dove,
  To the mountains of God's love;
Hide me in the clefted rock,
  From the world's wild tempest shock—
Seal me, Christ, Thy very own,
  Anchor me fast to the throne.
Shown myself, I fled away,
  Out of night into the day;
Shown my Lord, I now desire
  Heart and brain be set on fire,
Just to do the Master's will—
  When death comes, to praise Him still.
I am weak, but Thou art strong—
  Bear me through the pressing throng
Of life's cares and bitter grief;
  Let me ever find relief,
Looking to the heights sublime,
  Just beyond the shores of time.

Drop into my life, sweet trust,
　Write my name among the just;
Make me pure in heart, my King,
　And Thy praises I will sing,
While supplies of grace come down,
　Guiding me from cross to crown.

Treasures.

THE fair pictured face of my boy,
　The robes that are folded away,
The playthings that never are used,
　Since our darling grew tired of play.

A little red cup, with the seal
　Of little red lips on its rim,
Two worn shoes, where pretty white feet
　Like pretty white mice crept in.

A tress of brown hair that was cut
　From the locks of my sweet baby son;
A short little mound where he sleeps,
　Since his beautiful life is done.

But of all my treasures, the best
   Is my treasure laid up in heaven,
Where my baby is waiting for me,
   Till life's silver cord be riven.

In fancy I oft hear the rush
   Of swift angel wings as they come;
I linger, and long for the call
   That summons the tired mother home.

Soaring and Singing.

ONCE walking in the meadow ground,
   Just at the break of day,
The hush unbroken by a sound,
   The sky half pearl, half gray,
The rank lush grasses were empearled
   With heavy drops of dew—
One might have thought this big round world
   Just made, it seemed so new;

When, swift there whirled up from my feet
   A yellow breasted lark;
So God had kept you safe, my sweet,
   Through all the hours of dark;

SONGS OF HOPE.

And now you raise a matin hymn,
    Still singing as you fly;
I lose you in the distance dim,
    Against the morning sky.

But liquid notes come falling down,
    That soothe my heart to rest;
I weave the music in my crown,
    Dear little yellow breast.
My soul shall learn from you to sing,
    For I am soaring too;
And to the Father I will bring
    The trust I learned from you.

Soaring and singing all the time,
    I higher, higher rise;
And weave the measure into rhyme,
    To drop adown the skies.
O may it lodge along the ways,
    Teach other hearts to sing,
Until the earth is filled with praise,
    Until the heavens shall ring.

God sometimes stirs the heart with pain
    To find a hidden sweet;
The fountain pierced will rise again,
    To flow around His feet.

Sometimes the sweetest song you hear
    Comes from a bleeding heart;
The major notes are full of cheer,
    The minor make tears start.

You crush the rose for its perfume—
    God knows what he's about,
And, if He put us in the fire,
    At last will take us out.
Even the diamond must be cut
    To make its luster shine,
And gold itself will show but dim
    Until it is refined.

Day is Breaking.

SING, sing, sing, O break ye into singing,
The heavens and the earth will very soon be ringing;
I am looking up on high, and the portals of the sky
Will swing upon their hinges to let the King go by.

Praise, praise, praise, O break ye into praising,
The multitude in glory their triumph hymn are raising;
I seem to catch the rhyme, while my soul is beating time
With the measure of the music, and the sky begins to shine.

Wait, wait, wait, oh weary not in waiting,
There is promise of the morning, the day will soon be breaking;
So up and trim your light, the east is growing bright,
The rosy day is coming, to drive away the night.

Watch, watch, watch, I hear the Master calling,
And all adown the spaces the dust of stars is falling;
The armies of the sky are marshaling on high,
"Behold the bridegroom cometh," O don't you hear the cry?

Pray, pray, pray, bend down unto your praying,
The spicy winds of heaven are 'round about you playing;
The gateways are ajar, naught can his purpose bar,
'T is the glinting and the gleaming of Bethlehem's old star.

A Lump of Clay.

ONLY a little lump of clay,
    And it lies in the potter's hand;
He looks at it, he looks at the wheel,
With its burnished edge of sharpened steel,

Knows how the cruel touch will burn,
Yet will hold it down and turn and turn;
Then turn and turn with a loving touch—
The clay will break if ground too much.

A well shaped vase made from the clay,
Again 't is poised on the master's hand;
"Good wheel, I praise thee for thy share,
But, little vase, there is more to bear.
Thrust into the flames that brightly glow—
A mighty breath on the fires doth blow—
Dost think me a master hard and stern,
As I thrust you in to burn and burn?"

Would you know it now for the lump of clay
That lately lay on the potter's hand?
The flames grew cool, and he drew it out,
Lovingly then he turned it about.
The fire had given an added grace,
You knew by the smile on the master's face;
What if the vase had not held still
While the cruel fires did all their will?

Once but a lump of moistened clay,
That the potter could toss from his hand;
Now it is touched with the royal dyes
That mock earth's bloom and mirage the skies.

You might almost think the bird would soar
Out from the vase and up from the door;
A monarch's hall it is fit to grace,
Since it felt the wheel and the fire's embrace.

Man is only a lump of clay,
Till the Master Potter takes him in hand;
To-morrow will come, to-day will go,
The bud of the rose begins to blow.
Then wheel of my fate, you may turn and turn,
And fires of love, you may burn and burn;
Some must command and some must obey—
God is the potter, and I am the clay.

Only Leaves.

MY beautiful four years old darling
   Came pattering in one day;
"O mamma! I want to go gather
   For you a lovely boquet;
I will whisper down to the posies,
   And they'll whisper up to me—
And, mamma, won't that be funny?
   I'm as happy as I can be!"

Away ran my brown haired darling;
   My cup was full with its joy;
God was so good and so loving,
   To give me this precious boy—
Good, though He take my baby
   Back into His bosom again;
I would trust through the night of my sorrow,
   Shall the clay of the potter complain?

The sun was braiding a pattern
   Of checkered shadow and gold;
As it sifted atween the vine leaves—
   And here is my laddie so bold,
With posies so sweet for mamma.
   I gathered them out from his hand,
And bent to kiss the smiling mouth
   Of my baby from heaven's land.

I heeded his innocent prattle,
   How "the flowers were all in bed,"
And how he "could not wake them up,"
   So he "brought me some leaves instead."
Yes, only leaves, with here and there
   A common and worthless weed;
I felt no lack, my sweet boy's love
   Had filled my heart's deep need.

He wanted to please me, and I took
   His loving thought for me, as though
He had brought me the rarest blossoms
   My God could cause to blow.
And so methinks the Father,
   If we go with a handful of leaves,
Will kiss us upon the mouth, and judge
   By the love that each inweaves.

Thinking and Acting.

PEOPLE are thinking the grandest thoughts,
   That somebody yet must work out;
I thank the man that sows the seed,
   And rejoice when the reapers shout.
The world is our field, and we enter in,
For a fight with the deadly weeds of sin;
But whether we sow or whether we reap,
May Satan never find us asleep.

If we could think till our hair grew white,
Yet sit in our chair from morn till night,
Would the world grow richer for all the care,
Or honor us more for our silvery hair?

No; every thought must have its wing,
As every bird has its song to sing;
The bud is a promise, the flower the deed
To prove the quality of the seed.

If I am the thinker, O find me feet
To run and perform my errands sweet;
We all are not Christ's, whose garment's hem
Will heal the disease of soul-sick men;
But while we pour in the oil and the wine,
'T is the hidden thought makes the action fine;
I may give the beggar a crust, and he
May forget the crust, yet remember me.

Each action may hold so much of love,
'T will change to the guise of a holy dove.
There are naked to clothe and hungry to feed;
If we may not reap, we can sow the seed.
There are babies who need a mother's breast,
Mourners to comfort who long for rest;
There are tears to wipe and hands to hold,
Though the ones we loved are still and cold.

Foreshadowings.

WHAT do you think old Moses saw,
    When he climbed up Pisgah's mountain?
Was it only a glimpse of the promised land,
With her vine-clad slopes and shining sand,
    And the splash of some sparkling fountain?

And what do you think God's children see,
    As they stand in the rift of the ages?
Is it only a view of the stormy sky,
Or do they hear the Bridegroom's cry,
    Foretold by saints and sages?

"There is no change," the scoffers say,
    "The promise of Christ's coming
Is but a myth; the Lord's asleep,
And does not hear His children weep;"
    And this their feeble summing.

Look up, weak saints, the skies will break—
    I feel Him drawing nearer;
For all the forecasts of to-day
But tell us He is on the way—
    The heavens are growing clearer.

Transition times are these, my friends—
    We stretch from grace to glory;
I trim my lamp and lift it high,
    For well I know the Lord draws nigh;
    Then sing the old new story.

Beside the Stream.

I SAT on the western shore of the stream,
    The sun and my life were both running low;
The shimmering waves ran on like a dream,
    And rythmic winds were beginning to blow.
The sunshine and waves met in sweet embrace—
    My thoughts were like shallops run out to sea—
To the westering sky I turned my face,
    And the past, like echoes, came back to me.

The low, sweet ring of a silvery bell,
    That swung and rung in my childhood's time,
When violets worked with their fragrant spell,
    And my heart kept beat to the bell's clear chime.
The fever ran high in my eager youth,
    Ambition's sharp goad was pricking me on,
While mother was pointing the way of truth;
    And now I look back on some victories won.

Oh magical tints when the skies are blue,
　　When the pulse beats high and the brain is clear;
When we trust in man and trust God too,
　　While amaranths crown each rolling year.
But the rolling years came freighted with pain,
　　And death dug pits just under my feet;
My soul stood bare in a pitiless rain,
　　And I tasted of gall for every sweet.

But now let me sit by the still river side,
　　The sunshiny hills are not far away;
My fancies sail out on a luminous tide,
　　To anchor at last in heaven's broad bay.
The roses that budded and never had bloom,
　　I will gather beyond the dark river;
The hopes that rose bright and set in the tomb,
　　Will be mine in God's golden forever.

A Song by the Wayside.

I AM traveling over a thorny way,
　　Higher and higher I climb,
Out of the darkness and into the day,
　　My toil, my tears are sublime.

There are wounds for my hands and stings for my feet,
    Yet upward and onward I go;
The iron of pain in my soul cutteth deep,
    God smiteth me blow after blow.

He is carving his saint, I dare not complain,
    But look to my risen Lord;
This fight of affliction I yet must maintain—
    Find strength in his cross and his word.

The milestones that guide to the city of God,
    Are the graves where my darlings lie;
The faces I kissed are under the sod;
    What I loved cannot ever die.

Sweet Jesus went down through the gate of the tomb,
    Rose crowned with triumph and glory;
All the Christ's children must enter its gloom,
    In heaven we'll tell the sweet story.

Of the wonderful way God took us o'er,
    Till we changed our cross for our crown;
Methinks I'm nearing that sun steeped shore,
    Where I'll lay my burdens down.

Then smite me, dear Father, but love me still,
    Give strength for each added blow;
Let me only desire to do thy will,
    For thy way is right I know.

The coward flesh may shrink and may moan,
    The soul will look up with a smile;
The shore winds of heaven have over me blown,
    I'll anchor safe after awhile.

Down in the Trenches.

DOWN in the trenches, and lightning leaped from
    the throat of the guns;
The thunder of battle was bursting over our husbands
    and sons;
Down in the hell of the trenches, thick with their
    sulphurous smoke,
Where many a lad kissed death on the mouth, and
    many a brave heart broke.
Whether blue or gray was the jacket, the man that it
    covered lay still;
No blast of the bugle could rouse him, no whiz of the
    bullet could thrill;
Up from the grime of the trenches, white souls were
    climbing some height,
With the pean of victory sounding, these heroes went
    out of the fight.
If God has care for the sparrows, that fall in the
    woodland or plain,

Will he take no thought for the brave men, cut down
    like the ripened grain?
He gathers His jewels from trenches, as well as the
    down softened bed;
The man proved a hero while living, is no less a hero
    when dead.
Aye, soldiers, I look in your faces—those eyes show a
    flash like the steel;
The memory of the warlike days has fastened you with
    their seal.

I knew boys that went from the hearthstone, up from
    the mother's knee,
To wear the blue and beat the drum, the tocsin of
    the free;
I have known them borne out of the battle, wounded
    and spent with pain;
For them the reveille hath sounded—they never saw
    mother again.

    Sound a pean for the heroes
        Underneath the meadow grasses;
      For the boys that now are resting
        In the gaps of mountain passes.
      Blue bird, lark and red breast robin,
        Drop your songs as you fly over

Lowly mounds, where men are hidden,
   'Neath the scented crimson clover.
All ye winds so softly blowing,
   Rustle wheat and wild wood blossom,
Mother earth is very tender
   To the babes within her bosom.
Lincoln flashed some milk-white roadway,
   Out of pain and into glory;
Garfield's life burned out with fever,
   Like some tragic, frightful story.
All the way from plain to headland,
   Bells were ringing joy or sorrow;
Tears were falling, prayers were rising,
   God was ruling each to-morrow.
Wreaths of bay for statesman soldiers,
   Wreaths of flowers for all the others;
Men who dared to die for country,
   Crown them, crown them, men and brothers.
Tears may change to pearls and diamonds,
   Cries of pain to joyous singing;
When God musters out His army,
   Heaven's vallies will be ringing.
Men are proud of banners tattered,
   Won in stress and strain of battle;
Comrades falling, columns shattered,
   And for music, cannon's rattle.

Hark! I hear some bugle blowing!
Winds from somewhere coming, going,
Set the tattered flags aflying,
Till we fain would cease our crying
To admire the rythmic wonder.
Fired by battle's stormy thunder,
I, the poet of the soldier,
Rise to measure grander, bolder;
Triumph in each note is ringing,
Peace inspires my gladsome singing.
Clouds retire, the battle's over
For our boys beneath the clover.
Roses blow and bees are humming;
Down some future I see coming
Ranks of victors out of glory:
This shall end my soldiers' story.

Flowers and Women.

I STROLLED into a shady dell,
   There found a flower and loved it well;
A modest blue, dewy and sweet—
Had one but crushed it 'neath his feet.

The perfume from its grassy bed
Would mutely say, "The flower is dead—"
A voiceless, yet a powerful prayer,
Floating to heaven on the air.

I climbed upon the mountain top,
The winds were still, the sun was hot;
I found upon the mountain's cone
A royal bloom, left all alone.

Its cup was gold, the robe of flame,
Yet from its heart no perfume came;
I turned me from the gaudy show,
And left it for the winter's snow.

Two grades of women here behold—
The gracious type, the grandly cold;
One lives to bless, and one to show
Her colors, waving to and fro.

One is the sunlight of a home,
The other, meteor like, will come,
And flash athwart your summer sky—
But meteors only blaze, then die.

Wise men will gather to their breast
What promises content and rest;

The gentle voice, the graceful mien,
Are more than robings of a queen.

Fine gold will wear for many a year,
The tinsel ever proves most dear.
If women to themselves were true,
We'd often see the gown of blue.

The Midnight Cry.

DEAD! Our soldier, our chief and our friend,
    Oh, birds, stay your singing to-day;
Of hoping and praying can this be the end?
    A voice whispers back to me, nay.

The River of Death rolls its waves
    In a flood, close up to our feet;
We are weary of walking 'mong graves,
    Our hearts they so heavily beat.

Oh, Death, you have shadowed our land,
    Grim Monster, both cruel and bold;
We are powerless to loosen your hand,
    You grasp with a purpose to hold.

Midnight. Underneath the stars,
Death is letting down the bars;
Midnight. Hear the bridegroom's cry,
Ring adown the parted sky;
Swiftly soars the loosened soul,
Underneath the church bells toll;
Sad and solemn sounds they ring—
,Higher up the angels sing.
Our Chief has heard the Master's call—
For us the wormwood and the gall.

Ah, bells, you ring a ghastly lie—
Our Garfield was not born to die;
He broke the fretted leash of pain,
You cannot call him back again;
Beyond the stars he speeds away,
Out from the midnight into day;
Then mourning bells, ring soft and low—
You sadly tell a nation's woe.
I strive to follow with my eye,
This soul that speeds beyond the sky;
Follow a soul? 't were easier far
To behold the wind, or grasp a star.
Mother, your "baby" is not dead—
He's gone to live with God, instead.

True wife, if love will give you ease,
Behold a nation on its knees ;
Your grief is ours, and while we weep,
Christ giveth His beloved sleep.
Freed spirit, let me say good night,
And speed you in your upward flight ;
But in some other clime I'll say,
Good morning, friend, 'tis break of day.
The midnight gloom has passed along,
Creation wakes to sing her song.

Easter Hymn.

CHRIST has risen!   Hear the cry!
　　Leave the earth and climb the sky ;
Christ has risen! angels sing,
"Joy of earth and heaven's King."
Easter morning bursts her bars,
Christ has soared above the stars ;
Lo, the stone is rolled away—
Night has given place to day.

Powerless watch and seal and stone—
Christ *must* rise, His work is done;
Only angels bide within,
Christ has triumphed o'er our sin.
Weeping Mary, dry your tears—
Christ is risen— dismiss your fears;
Pure white lilies haste to bring—
Help the seraphs while they sing.

Christ has risen! Soul grow white;
Christ arose, my path is light;
May He lead me all the way,
Ever near Him let me stay.
When the trump of God shall sound,
Rousing nations underground,
Victor over death and sin,
Immortality I'll win.

Coming Home.

A HAPPY mother called this morn
   Across the alley way,
" Good morning, neighbor, I am glad
   'T is such a pleasant day,

For Charlie's coming home, you see,
   He has been gone so long,
This morning when I left my bed
   My lips took up a song;
It quite surprised the mocking bird,
It was so long since he had heard
   His mistress' voice so merrrily;
Our house is silent as the grave.
     When both the boys are gone away
     What can the mother do but pray?"

Ah, neighbor, you have struck a chord
   That vibrates in my heart,
It fills me with a sudden pain,
   And makes the hot tears start,
For both *my* boys are gone away,
   They left their mother's breast;
How can a mother bear to sing
   With but an empty nest?

But when the boys are coming home,
The song and smile are quick to come;
How oft I stand and shade my eyes,
Looking away toward the skies,
   Eager to catch some little sign
   That God will send concerning mine.

Why should I look the way they went?
    That will not bring them back ;
My boys have gone to see the King,
    Along a shining track ;
But they are coming home again,
    I'll set the house all right,
For who can tell but what *my* lads
    Are coming home to-night.
And when I hear the trumpet blow,
To greet them swiftly will I go,
And welcome them with smile and song,
My boys who have been gone so long ;
    Then open wide both heart and door,
    Our sons are coming home once more.

A Winter Idyl.

THE wind is tapping at my door,
    With dim, uncertain feeling ;
He whispers some wierd ancient lore,
    That to my ears is stealing.
Gray clouds are trooping o'er the sky,
The storm is coming by and by,
While clouds are marshaling on high,
    The wind harps still keep pealing.

The winds blow east and winds blow west,
    The birds are homeward flying,
As I fly to my Father's breast,
    In living or in dying.
When lightnings flash and thunders roll,
It is the signal for my soul
To quickly seek her sure, safe goal,
    Where Christ will still my crying.

Here comes a dash of icy rain,
    Against my window drumming;
Nature is stirred by some swift pain,
    And so her tears are coming.
Nature and hearts must have their way,
The sky will clear some other day,
We must endure while skies are gray—
    This is my hasty summing.

Some rain comes down like drops of balm,
    So gentle and refreshing;
Some lives are full of summer calm,
    Burned with the sun's hot blessing;
Yet lives drink tears like showers of rain
Only to bud and bloom again,
Or else stand thick with golden grain,
    To woo the wind's caressing.

Peace and Good Will.

A CHRISTMAS carol I joyously sing,
   Of the beautiful long ago,
The heavenly arches then did ring,
   With a song, whose musical flow
Adown the grand old aisle of years
   Has drifted even till now;
It calls for smiles, it calls for tears—
   Wreathes glory around the brow;
'T is peace on earth, good will to men,
A glorious theme for human pen.

One beautiful night when the stars were out,
   And shepherds were watching their flocks,
The angels came down with a ringing shout,
   Heaven's odors in their bright locks;
They came to chant a cradle hymn
   For the baby just given to earth.
No distance or time can ever dim,
   The lullaby sung at that birth;
'T was peace on earth good will to men,
Too grand a theme for human pen.

Did the wise men walking over the hill,
   Their eyes on the guiding star,
Feel the soul within them throb and thrill,
   As they heard the song from afar?

Knew they heaven was near that night,
    To Bethlehem's humble town?
Methinks a stable's aglow with light,
    Since the Lord of glory came down
With his peace on earth, good will to men,
Inspiring the human heart and pen.
I wonder, did Mary raise up her head,
    While holding the child to her breast?
(No matter to her how lowly the bed,
    She was Mary, 'mong women most blest).
Heard she the song that is filling the earth,
    And filling the heavens as well?
Did the heavenly choir fathom its worth,
    Or know the wonderful spell
That is hidden in peace, good will to men,
Melting the heart and ruling the pen?
I fancy that over celestial heights
    The angels are now looking down,
A glorious smile each face uplights;
    I catch the rich gleam of a crown,
And just beyond, I see the dear face,
    The luminous face of my King.
Glory comes down to fill this place,
    The heavenly arches ring
With peace on earth, good will to men,
Sung over to-night yet once again.

My Lesson.

NATURE is teaching me lessons so sweet,
   Here is the one she taught me to day:
The sunshine was melting around my feet,
   But up to the mountains I took my way;
Down in the valleys the winds were still,
   Lillies were panting for breaths of air,
But breezes were blowing up on the hill,
   And I was going to hunt them there.

Winds that were shaking the giant tree,
   Blown in from the ocean, out from the west,
Where breakers were riding their white horses free,
   Tossing the ships lightly up on each crest.
Ah, souls that are lapsed in the summer time's calm,
   Who have no need for a shelter or shield;
Whose days are set to some low, tender psalm,
   What of the souls that God blows afield?

What of the blossoms hid under the snow,
   Crimson and white, yet they never have birth;
Yet the winds of God blow high and blow low,
   From shore unto shore across the broad earth.

When winds roar loudest the oaks take root,
　　When fires are hottest the gold will shine;
The pruned trees bear the finest fruit,
　　Round lightning scarred trunks the ivy will twine.

If life were a calm, and never a breeze
　　Blew in from eternity's sea,
Humanity never would fall on its knees,
　　Or long for the life giving tree.
The vintage is ripened by winds and the sun,
　　The clusters of grapes turn to wine;
And the lesson that I from the hill tops have won,
　　I must master it line upon line.

Rizpah.

COULD the brush of a Raphael paint the scene?
　　Could he put on canvas a mother's pain?
Can our thoughts so subtle grasp the theme,
　　And thus picture it over again?
Till a listening world shall catch the chime
Of this story lived in the olden time.

In a rocky gorge far up Judea's hills,
 Where mountain winds blow coolly, purely through,
The sombre picture grows—our hearts it thrills
 With pathos old and yet forever new;
Swinging against the sky are Rizpah's boys,
What careth Rizpah now for life's poor joys?

See! There upon the barren rock she stands,
 Beating the hungry vultures from their prey;
Her heart is aching, bleeding are those hands,
 And yet she keeps the fierce eyed birds at bay;
The orient night drops down, and bears along
The faint, wierd echoes of her wailing song.

Through all the solemn night she watches there,
 Her two sons gently swinging to and fro,
The prowling beast she drives back to his lair,
 And thus the night wears on, sadly and slow;
The rosy morning sweeps aside her veil,
 Yet still goes on poor Rizpah's mournful wail.

Her purplish hair unbound, the mountain air
 Toys roughly with it, and anon her eyes,
So late grown heavy with her pain and care,
 Are like a jungle tiger's, those fierce cries
Menace her silent treasures swinging there,
E'en death itself, the mother love would dare.

For five long dreary months she watched her dead,
    This Hebrew mother in the olden time,
And since those days how many hearts have bled,
    How many souls climbed up the heights of time,
Pain carving out the steps from earth to God,
For all He loves must pass beneath the rod.

Poor broken hearted ones who weep to-day,
    Over an empty cradle, look above ;
Your darlings have gone up a royal way,
    And all the track is silvered o'er with love ;
But ah, our eyes are blind with many tears,
    We have no strength to climb, clogged with our fears.

Why should you fear? yet you *must* climb, or miss
    The babes that slipped away from your strong hold ;
A stronger drew the ones you loved to kiss,
    And now they safely rest within the fold.
Rizpah's two sons went up, and so have mine ;
I'm searching for them, and I still must climb.

Crayon Sketches.

A FAIR young mother looked with pain
   On the face of her suffering child;
"Oh, what shall I do for my little one,
   My heart with anguish is wild!
Here comes a friend that will tell me how
   To give you speedy relief,
Then mamma's tears will change to smiles—
   Now my heart is wrung with grief."
"O, give the baby a weak gin sling,
   It is only the cholic, my dear,
I have always found it was just the thing
   For *my* babies, so be of good cheer."
Young mother you play with a dangerous toy,
This whisky toddy may ruin your boy.

The lovely babe was grown to a lad
   Who came running in one day;
"My son, your cheeks are so hotly flushed,
   You work too hard at your play."
"No mother, its not the play this time,
   You see, Mr. A., on the street,
Took me in the saloon with a pleasant smile,
   And gave me a little treat;

I believe he called it lager beer,
  'T was a filthy, bitter drink,
And, mamma, my head, it feels so queer,
  As if I could hardly think."
The wind was sown in years agone,
And lo, the whirlwind sweepeth on.

Along the street walked a stalwart man,
  The dew of youth in eye, on brow,
But a serpent is coiling within his brain,
  He fights the monster with throes of pain,
Yet tighter and closer grows the strain;
  The tempter conquers—he yieldeth now.
" Yes, give me wine to quench my thirst,
  I will drink and be merry to-day;
Red wine, they tell me you are a curse,
  I remember how mother would pray,
O, keep my boy from a drunkard's fate,
  But now the siren has sung her song;
The spell's upon me, too late, too late !
  To the fatal plunge I am whirled along,"
  To my listening ear was an echo given,
It came from above, " No drunkards in Heaven,"

A man grown old before his time,
  Is stretched on his couch to die;

My blood grows cold, I shudder with fear,
   As I list to the agonized cry :
" Why don't you beat back those fiends of hell?
   They are tearing my heart from my breast,
Have pity I pray, my brain is on fire,
   O, I am so tired, let me rest.
My life is a wreck, so heart, beat your last,
   I will speed me away in the night;
What is it I hear? my poor mother's prayer,
   Strong drink turned my steps from the right."
A quivering heap sank down in the bed,
The victim of rum before me lay dead.

Sleep.

I HEARD the soft beating of wings,
   As the angel of sleep swept down,
She bore me away to a lovely land,
   And she laid on my brow a crown.

There was healing and peace in the touch,
   The fountain of joy in my breast
Sprang like a lark from the meadow grass,
   My soul half unclothed was at rest.

Cherished things that had slipped from my hold,
　　Came to me in this wonderful land,
The baby I kissed when his lips were cold,
　　Tenderly clung again to my hand.

My mother came vestured in light,
　　The pain all gone out of her eyes,
She had caught a raptured, glorified look,
　　From her dwelling place in the skies.

We talked of the woes overpast,
　　Of the triumph she lately had won,
We rejoiced, and we gave all the praise
　　To Jesus, God's crucified son.

I seemed to be drifting away
　　From my vision so rare and so sweet :
I woke to my cares, yet was glad to think
　　My loved were in Jesus asleep.

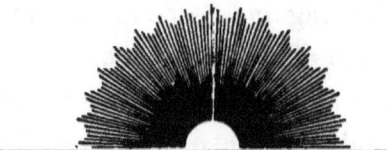

Little Brown Hen.

THE little brown once wanted to crow,
The little brown hen could not make it go,
 Oh, dear, dear-a-me.
What was the reason, do you suppose?
The crow in her throat was almost froze—
 It did n't come free.

"She hasn't a voice, that's pretty clear,"
Shouted the rooster into my ear;
 The rooster is wise.
What shall I do with the little brown hen?
Make a pot pie for eloquent men
 To praise to the skies.

I made the little brown hen a nest,
Put plenty of eggs beneath her breast,
 But that did'nt please.
She preferred to go in the storm and wet,
The little brown hen wasn't ready to set;
 She flew to the trees.

There she essayed a wonderful crow;
The rooster, down on the ground below,
 Cried, "Try it again."
The little brown hen flew into a rage—
"I tell you, I'm as fit for the stage,
 And have as much brain

"As any pert rooster; you know it is true.
It is perfectly easy to cock-doodle-doo—
　　Now just hear me try."
The young hen's grandmother now drew near;
"Come out of the tree, my pretty dear—
　　How well you can fly.

You see there is plenty of work to do,
The question of crowing need not trouble you;
　　'T is only a noise.
I think the hens do as much good, or more,
As many roosters that strut 'round the floor,
　　To be aped by boys.

"You had better attend to your nest and eggs,
For in them are beaks and long yellow legs,
　　To crow in due time.
You and the rooster each have a place,
'T is doubtful which will win in the race,
　　Each in your own line.

"God made a difference in His plan
Betwixt the woman and the man;
　　And here is the rest:

　　He made the woman last, my dear,
　　So to my mind it is pretty clear
　　　　The woman is best."

Indian Summer is Dead.

THE Indian Summer Maid, with purple tinted hair,
With her wealth of golden fruit, that scented all
the air;
With her silver harvest moon set swinging in the sky,
Has hid herself away from me, nor answers to my cry.
She kissed the whispering trees till they blushed in
gold and red—
My pretty Indian Maiden, she surely must be dead;
She dashed her ruby wine into the hazy air,
And the glory of her presence still lingers everywhere.
Old Winter, grim and gloomy, sits howling o'er her
grave—
I see him tear his whitened hair, and hear him wildly
rave;
The brown and frightened birdies have hidden from
his grief—
One pities Father Winter, but cannot give relief.
But our little Indian girl will surely come again—
We'll watch for her in April days, and through the
Summer rain;
When the Autumn glory comes we will hear her gentle
tread,
For God will keep His promise, and raise her from
the dead.

Love.

O LOVE is the lever that moveth the world,
God's mercy forever to man is unfurled;
Sweet winds, tell the story and move it along,
Fill earth with His glory and help swell the song.

Yes, love is the chorus the angels will sing,
The heavens spread o'er us will joyously ring;
The lips of the mother with love are abloom—
Let us love one another from cradle to tomb.

Love breathes on the roses until they flush red,
'T is heard in the closes sung over the dead ;
'T is the wonderful fashion that Jesus brought down,
The sign of God's passion, which ends with a crown.

The blessed Evangel once given to earth,
A flaming white angel that heralds new birth—
Love hopeth and beareth when stung by the rod,
Sure that somebody careth, and that love is God.

Broken Shackles.

ONE Wilberforce went up to heaven,
    With broken fetters in his hand,
He suffered long, he lived and died,
    But grandly blessed his native land.

And evermore 'round England's shore,
    Methinks is girt a belt of glory,
For unborn nations he will write
    In golden lines again his story.

All may not win this road to bliss,
    But each can give the widow's mite;
'Tis love brings down the scale of God,
    He counts our deeds sitting in light.

Our Lincoln flashed the milky way,
    That hangs betwixt our souls and bliss;
Three million shackles in his hand,
    And Jesus met him with a kiss.

On Calvary the savior died,
    And laid before his Father's throne
The chains from off a world of slaves—
    The lily of God's love had blown.

Down in the noisome slums of life
   I see so many hands uplift,
All chained; a cloud broods over them
   Its inky folds without a rift.

These drunkards left to die and rot,
   Like carrion on God's royal earth;
Where is the man to do, to dare,
   And give them back the freeman's birth?

So many hands beat at these chains,
   Until their own are bruised and sore,
And yet they hold, deep festering in,
   As years go by, it seems the more.

They eat the lives, the souls of men;
   Our eagle flyeth low and slow.
It tires its wings to drag this load,
   Aye, cut him loose and let him go.

Up, till he looks God in the face,
   Fearless, and stays his restless flight,
Freedom, thrice won, will hail the world;
   Our land must climb towards the right.

Warp and Woof.

ONE sweet thought wanders through
  The chambers of my brain ;
I catch the glint of silver wings,
  Like the mist of summer rain.

Out of sorrow, out of care,
  Life brings unto our door,
We may weave a glorious robe
  To wear when life is o'er.

Grieving and pain, the warp ;
  The woof, God's wondrous grace ;
The rare design we'll comprehend,
  When we see the Father's face.

Now a jewel is inwrought,
  Anon a jet gleams forth ;
Set it around with gems of light,
  And make it of priceless worth.

The sharpest pain may bring
  The purest joy at last;
Under the gray the sun shines still,
  Though the sky be overcast.

'T is a wondrous web we weave;
   The shuttle flies day and night,
The weaver speeds away, away,
   To the land of boundless light.

Then gather silver and gold,
   For you the robe shall wear,
In the heavenly courts before the King,
   And in all his glory share.

The Mother's Lament.

'T IS only a little girl that has fled,
   Out of our home and away from our sight;
They tell me our dear little Ruth is dead,
   That our darling has turned her face to the light.

Only six years old, but how she had grown
   Into our lives and into our love;
Now I stand here beside her making my moan,
   And still she sleeps on, poor, tired little dove.

Baby, wake up, for mamma has come,
   To gather her girlie up to her breast;
Unheeded the call, to our grief she is dumb,
   These lips are so cold my warm ones have pressed.

My brain madly whirls, yet my eyelids are dry,
    Could weeping assuage a sorrow like mine?
So far from me gone, and yet she is nigh,
    Sweet Father above, she is mine—she is thine.

Yes, I *am* her mother, and Ruthie is free
    From sin, pain and weeping, her conflict is o'er;
The gift was divine, I commit her to Thee,
    Till I claim her again on eternity's shore.

I'll smoothe back the hair from the broad white brow,
    And kiss the closed eyes whence the sunshine has fled;
Frail hands—they cannot hug dear mamma now,
    Quiet feet—yes, John, our loved one is dead.

How lovely she is—too fair for the tomb,
    Too sweet for our holding, and so she has gone;
Ever more in our hearts is one empty room,
    Till we hail her again in heaven's bright dawn.

John, strong was the tie that bound us before,
    Grief is the rivet to tighten the link;
Good bye, little one, our grieving is sore,
    The spirit is willing yet the bruised heart will shrink.

Hagar.

PRELUDE.

BRING down the pathos of the old,
   Into the heart of the new;
One half the story has not been told,
The mines of the past are rich with gold,
   Yet nothing but God is true.

Ever we hear the dull refrain
   Of men and women who grieve;
The burden of life is passion and pain,
   Poor fettered hearts have tugged at their chain
Since the days of Adam and Eve.

HAGAR.

She stood in the door of the tent
   In the cool of the day;
In the cool of the early morning
   Hagar was sent away
   With her gift of bread and water.
   And she held by the hand
Her boy, while their faces were turned
   Toward the desert land.

Yes, out from the folds of the tent
   That long had been her home,
She and the child were going,
   Never again to come.
Abraham stood in the shadow,
   Watching as they went out,
But Sarah stood in the sunlight—
   Sarah had never a doubt.

Yes, it was time they were going,
   Isaac was pressed to her heart,
And she stood with eyes ashining,
   Waiting to see them start.
Hagar turned once, and looked backward,
   Fierce as a tiger at bay,
And then she and Ishmael hurried
Over the toilsome way.

God was watching the wanderers
   Till gone were water and bread;
Hagar had cast the lad away,
   And mourned for him as dead.
She sat her down a long way off,
   Wringing her empty hands ;
God had forgotten, and they must die
   Out on these burning sands.

God! Where was God? She must find him,
   And tell him about the boy;
Would He shatter her life with one fierce stroke,
   Rob her of every joy?
That was *her* heaven out yonder,
   Going at one bold throw,
Madness assailed the tortured brain,
   She sank beneath the blow.

The voice of an angel calling,
   Water and life were sent;
One heart had stopped its crying
   For Abraham's sheltering tent.
When God makes a break with our pain,
   A blessing awaits at the sill;
To suffer is joy, to bear is strength,
   If at last comes, "Peace, be still."

Some mothers will fold their babies
   Into white beds each night,
While others are crying with Hagar,
   Blindly groping for light.
O, list to the angels calling,
   Poor hearts both heavy and sair,
But after the night comes morning,
   And Jesus your pain will bear.

The Day and I.

THE day is growing old, the sky is turning gray,
    It is growing old and gray, like myself;
The sun will soon go down, and night is coming on,
    To lay the day and me upon the shelf.

The day will not be dead, but her tender grace will
    come,
    To twine about my dreaming ever more;
Then I will lie and wait till the dreaming time is
    done—
    The day and I will waken when 't is o'er.

The rosy, dewy morn will all come back to me,
    The summer noon from out a summer sky;
And e'en the purple night, with misty, dreamy light,
    For beauty grown immortal will not die.

The lily of my love will be blowing once again,
    The bugle of my joy will be sounding:
The days are going home in a long and stately line,
    The head lands of glory they are rounding.

Belshazzer's Feast.

THE night had come down like a dove to its nest,
The stars of the East were aflame on her breast;
There was music and mirth in yon banqueting hall,
Where gathered the fairest and bravest of all.

A hundred lamps swung from the wall overhead,
O'er a thousand fierce lords was their bright splendor shed;
The golden cups blazed, the wine was aglow,
And smiles lent their charm to this barbaric show.

The king on his throne in the pride of his power,
Had visions of conquests to brighten the hour;
Too soon the joy changed to a shuddering dread,
And pale grew the cheeks that the wine had flushed red.

A strange hand gleamed from the tapestried wall,
And silence shut down like a funeral pall;
Those fingers quick wrote out in letters of fire,
For the Lord had come down "in the pomp of his ire."

The vessels of Judah dropped out from the hand,
And panic now ruled the once valiant band;
While the monarch cried out with a trembling awe,
For the wise men to read him the words which he saw.

Alas! all their wisdom was empty and vain,
Though they would they could not the meaning explain;
When a low voice like music crept into the air,
"My Lord, I entreat thee, yield not to despair.

"I know a poor captive from Israel's land,
Will tell thee what meaneth the mystical hand."
"Then, ho! have him in, and I will bestow
One third of my crown if the meaning he show."

Then Daniel stood up in the sight of them all,
And told them the sense of the words on the wall:
"The kingdom is rent from thy hand, and thy sword
To the Medes and the Persians I give," saith the Lord.

"Thou art weighed in the balance, found wanting, and now
I will take the diadem off from thy brow."
A hush filled the room—the tale it was told—
Ere morning Belshazzar was silent and cold.

Two guests uninvited—stern Death and the Lord—
Had come to the feast and spoken their word;
For singing and laughter came weeping and moan,
For the purple and crown were the shroud and the stone.

A Temperance Dream.

I SAT lazily rocking one day,
    As often a woman will,
When I fell asleep and seemed to be
    Up-climbing a fearful hill.
There I was met by a grizzly shape
    No mortal could ever describe;
'Twas clothed in tatters from head to foot—
    A beggar the garb would deride.

I gasped, " Will you please to tell your name,.
    And if ever we've met before?"
" I am Statistics," and then the thing
    Uttered a hideous roar.
" Ay, you are quite harmless, I see,
    But you help to fill up a bill;
You have been fired again and again—
    You may cripple, but never can kill."

" I can tell the drink bill of the world,
    How many are keeping saloons,
How many are dying from year to year
    From breathing hell's terrible fumes;

Of the widows that wring their hands,
    The orphans that cry for bread,
In short, give figures for everything,
    All the way from the living to dead."

So I grew quite free with this shape,
    And asked if to me it could tell
How many souls went down in the storm
    That was raised by the owner of hell;
How many the tears that are shed,
    How many hearts broken by drink?
The puzzled wight then scratched his head,
    And answered, "I really can't think.

"Another man keeps those accounts,
    And he will be sure to know."
So I turned from the bloated thing—
    My steps were heavy and slow;
I stopped at the first black door—
    A gentle push opened it wide;
I walked adown the bright saloon,
    Till I stopped by the merchant's side.

"Sir, for those engaged in your trade,
    One is keeping a book, I'm told;
In these accounts, from day to day,
    Is marked every shipwrecked soul!

The tears that rum has caused to flow,
   The hearts he has broken, for aye;
Do you know the power that keeps the books,
   Noting items of Alcohol's sway?

"In these accounts perhaps you can tell
   The figures set down for you;
I am told the one that foots them up
   Is called ever faithful and true."
"Madam, I neither know, nor care—
   You had better be going your way;
The temperance folks are raising a muss,
   And we find there's the devil to pay."

"Yes, sir, you are right, and perhaps the bill
   Will make you open your eyes;
I have no desire, my honored sir,
   To share in the little surprise."
I turned from him and woke from my dream,
   But the battle I'll never give o'er;
Whisky I'll fight as long as I live,
   Then sail to heaven's fair shore.

We will load our cannon quite up,
   With the weight of the moral law,
And when it is fired at the enemy's ranks,
   Down will go their men of straw.

Then up to the ramparts, my men,
   And the flag of victory wave;
The Lord is leaning over the heights—
   The Lord, who the drunkard can save.

The car is coming, oh don't you hear
   The music that heralds its way?
Ah, when it is here we women will go
   Low down on our knees to pray.
And when at last we have stormed the fort,
   We will cheer till the heavens ring;
Never give up, though you die in the trench,
   For the future will victory bring.

The Two Brooks.

SHALL I tell you a story, David,
   The fairy queen whispered to me,
Of two little brooks that started
   To run away down to the sea?

One glided through grass and flowers,
   Sparkled and dimpled along,
The blue sky arched above it,
   And cheered by the wild bird's song.

One brook came down from the mountain,
    Through the granite carving its way;
The feet of green mosses crept softly
    To the water's brink in their play.

The brooks grew to full banked rivers,
    So deep, so rapid and free;
But whether in sun or in shadow,
    They crept straight along to the sea.

Their waters in one were blended,
    As the night melts into the day;
Sun and stars smiled down on the union,
    Yet seaward they still kept their way,

Till they poured their united waters
    Into the breast of the sea.
The rose spills her cup of fragrance,
    Yet is happy as rose can be.

Thus with our lives, my David,
    They are gliding along the way,
Either in glow or in gloaming.
    Just twelve years ago to-day,

Since we braided them up together,
    To run their swift way to the sea,

Whose waters are pure as crystal —
 They are waiting for me and thee.

An ocean of love unfathomed,
 Where we lose our sorrow and care ;
The night never bends above it,
 And the day is eternally fair.

The Bridge o'er which the Babies Go.

LOW, dark hills on either side—
 Between them rushed a river;
Black and angry was the tide,
 Whose waves flow on forever.
Lined with wrecks are both the banks,
 The wind is filled with sighing,
And still they come in broken ranks,
 This army of the dying.

Feebly marching to the grave,
 I see them shrink and shiver ;
But thou dost stretch an icy wave
 To grasp them, cruel river.

No glint of sun to light the stream,
   No foam, white crested, flowing,
But like some endless nightmare dream,
   'T was always going, going.

Pour in the ruby wine of life,
   It mocks at moans and weeping—
The waves keep up their endless strife,
   Our treasures onward sweeping.
But how do all the babies go
   Across this stormy ocean?
They cannot stem the waves' swift flow
   And waters' wild commotion.

High above the whirling stream
Stretches out a shining beam,
   Like a holy vision;
O'er this highway of the air,
Passes every baby fair,
   Into realms elysian.

Passing swiftly, passing slow,
Babes and angels come and go,
   In and out of glory;
Robes of whiteness pass along—
Don't you hear a ringing song
   That tells a happy story?

"We have passed from pain and strife,
Stretched the elastic cord of life,
   But it is not broken ;
Deathless love shall ever reign,
You shall welcome us again,
   Christ our blessèd token.

"He built this bridge that we might run
Out of shadow into the sun,
   Above the ice cold river ;
If we grow tired upon the way,
His loving breast our heads will stay—
   Now are we happy ever."

This is the way the babies go,
Sweet as incense, white as snow,
   And yet our hearts are breaking;
But over on the other side,
Beyond the black and stormy tide,
   Our souls will soon be waking.

Nest Building.

THE birds are busy building nests,
    And mine is all torn down;
The winds may blow and skies drop rain—
I ne'er can build my nest again,
    For I'm a bird with a broken wing,
    And hardly have courage my song to sing.

How I pity the bird that cannot fly—
    That cannot build a nest;
When its fellows twitter and coo in spring,
It must drag along with a broken wing;
    No airy flight up into the tree,
    No building time for the bird or me.

The bird can sing, and so can I—
    Break into praise, O soul!
The saddest word in any tongue,
That was ever spoken, writ or sung
    Is, "It might have been;" the sweetest to me
    Are these brief words: "'T is sure to be."

I know the Lord will build for me,
  And heal my wounded wing ;
Yet I want again my ruined nest,
And the boys that lay upon my breast ;
  So my heart laments as I watch the birds,
  With a pain that cannot be put in words.

Baby's Poem.

MY baby he wrote a poem,
  That only the angels can read ;
I look on the characters half divine—
My heart is thrilled, for the boy was mine ;
I have sent him to school in a sunny clime,
  To learn the angels' creed.

This holy creed is only love,
  But the hardest of all to learn ;
Methinks I will sit at my darling's feet,
And learn the lesson with patience sweet,
While our hearts together as one will beat,
  And love divine will burn.

I said he *was* mine; dost think I mean
　　The Father has ta'en him away?
He *is* mine by every throb of pain,
He is part of myself in body and brain,
And the head that over my heart hath lain
　　God will give back some day.

Do you marvel at my simple faith?
　　Then wonder no longer my friend;
Methinks I have stood on Pizgah's mount,
My lips have quaffed from a holy fount—
The living and dying I do not count—
　　For bliss that crowns the end.

The mystery of my baby's song
　　I may yet read over at will;
But now it is like the wing of a dream,
That daintily brushed and dipped in life's stream,
While flashing along, it gave me a gleam
　　Of rapture, my heart to thrill.

The Twins.

IT is a sweet puzzle, I pray you to tell,
    Which one is Laura and which one is Floy;
I halfway think they are cheating us all,
    And there's only one girl to delude some boy.

A couplet in verse are these charming girls,
    A duet in music, you plainly can see;
One of them thinks she can make her own fate,
    The other, what's fated is certain to be.

Alas! how I pity the trusting lad,
    Who is happy enough one heart to win,
He never could tell if *this* were his wife,
    Or only her sister, the *other* sweet twin.

May Cupid assail the fort of each heart,
    May these twins be divided in twain;
King Love slay each girl with thy keen little dart,
    Yet kill them without any needless pain.

Twin peaches are rosy yet have but one stone,
    While each of these maids owns a heart;
Were I wiser I'd tell you just how it is done,
    Dividing these Siamese maidens apart.

Thoughts for Scientists.

THE cattle on the hills are his,
    The strong hills too,
They lift their green heads up to him:
    Why should not you?
Why boldly fling your impious thought
    Into the air,
And dare te say with bated breath,
    "God is not there!"

You glibly settle things and say:
    From atoms grew,
The great round world that swings in space,
    With all her crew.
Who hurled the primal molecule out,
    And gave the swing
That made the atom grow and flower
    In everything.

Pregnant with grandest meaning 't was,
    When brought to birth;
It gave force, matter, and even law,
    To rule this earth.

It gave to man the awful thought
  That conceived God,
O, lying atom! you deserve
  To feel the rod.

But who shall scourge? The thing evolved
  Looks up and dares,
Believe and trust a higher power,
  That answers prayers.
If you could only grow and give
  Unto our eyes,
The Maker that our hearts demand,
  And break the skies

To let a Christ come through, O, then
  We should be blest!
The tide of life heaves on and on,
  In search of rest.
But there *is* rest, for I have found
  My God at last.
Bold science I defy, and nail
  Truth to the mast.

The bed that science makes is short,
  It cramps me so;
The covers are too small for me,
  And I will go

In search of better things. Will you
    Journey with me?
At last we'll break through Time, and find
    Eternity.

Leaves from Gethsemane.

A BUNCH of dry and crumbling leaves,
    But round about them history weaves
  A wild, pathetic story;
Once they were plucked from olive trees,
    Kissed by an oriental breeze,
  And kissed, as well, by glory.

O, that my lips were touched by fire,
That I could strike some sounding lyre,
  And fill the earth with singing.
My eyes o'erflow with tears of praise,
And I a song of love will raise,
  Till earth and heaven are ringing.

Once underneath the olive's shade,
My Savior knelt, my Savior prayed,
  Heart broken with his sorrow;
No wonder should the spirit quail,
The cross, the thorns, the iron nail,
  Waited for Him to-morrow.

And so He lay upon the sod,
And raised His broken voice to God,
   "O, let the cup pass over."
The drops of blood upon his brow,
In fancy I can see them now;
   They seem to stain the clover.

A fancy; let me hold it, friend,
And even here it will not end;
   If the red clover's keeping
A stain of blood, why then the white
Was bleached upon that dreadful night,
   By His impassioned weeping.

O, Garden of Gethsemane,
Where watched the sorrow burdened three,
   And where these leaves were growing,
I sit and wonder at the love
That brought Christ Jesus from above—
   Such gifts on man bestowing.

For every one that will believe,
Shall everlasting life receive—
   The heavens and earth are ringing,
And everywhere the sweet winds blow,
This gift of God is sure to go—
   I cannot keep from singing.

God's Mercy.

I STOOD by the harbor of heaven,
   The sea lay shining and wide,
And over the harbor bar rolled
   The waves in an endless tide.
I wanted to touch the other shore,
   So my ships went sailing away;
To the north, the south, the east and west,
   They sailed for many a day.

As I sat beside the harbor bar,
   The waves came rolling along;
And as they broke I seemed to catch
   The echoing notes of song.
At last my ships came sailing back,
   I saw them from afar,
And shouted: "Have you found the shore?"
   Ere they reached the harbor bar.

"No shore, no shore," was the answering cry;
   "This ocean, it has no rim;
We found no place to anchor our boats,
   So we came to anchor with Him

Who holdeth creation in His hand;"
    Yet still I sent my cry,
"Found you any sunken rocks, brave lads,
    Where stranded wrecks might lie?"

"We never found a sunken rock,
    Though we sounded o'er and o'er;
We sailed north, south, to east and west,
    Yet never came to shore."
I praise thee, God, for this shoreless sea,
    Whose depths no plummet can sound;
It runs away in gleaming waves,
    And touches eternity's bound.

MISCELLANEOUS.

Maids and Apple Blossoms.

MAIDEN with the sunny eyes,
   Apple blooms to crown thy hair—
Standing now in mute surprise,
   Baptised in the spring time air;
Hast thou, maid, a snow white heart?
Rosy red when Cupid's dart,
Pierces it with guileless art?
   Tell me maiden if you dare,
   With apple blossoms in your hair.

See her shake that nut brown head—
   Flash upon me those blue eyes—
Some sweet magic from her sped;
   Yes, the maid seems very wise.

Singing like some mocking bird,
Yet one cannot catch a word,
Still the girl is not absurd.
    What knows she of pain or care,
    With apple blossoms in her hair?

Birds are mating in the tree;
    Hast found thy mate my little girl?
Surely now thou 'lt answer me;
    But I see the red lips curl.
Had I now thy pure heart's key,
I would set the rebel free,
Then chain it fast again to me.
    Thou art saucy, thou art fair,
    With apple blossoms in thy hair.

I 'd rather lock myself within,
    And fling the key away;
Thus the fortress I would win,
    And then no more would stray.
Ah, have I woke the ruby's glow,
Upon thy forehead's alpine snow?
Then, dainty rebel, you may go;
    Of joy and sport have thy full share,
    While apple blossoms crown thy hair.

A Soul at Auction.

WHO bids, who bids, for this little white soul,
    The soul of my darling child?
The World, the Flesh and the Devil uprise,
    Their eyes are eager and wild.

"I bid," said the World, "riches and show,
    For these man toils like a slave;
In the end a white marble shaft shall uprise,
    And gleam in the sun o'er a grave."

"I," said the Flesh," bid every delight
    That gratified Passion can give;
The present is thine; take thine ease, O, soul,
    I bid thee right merrily live."

The Devil cried out: "I bid these—yea more,
    Ambition and marvelous power;
We three are one firm, and I am the head;
    Soul, thou art mine from this hour."

A low voice rose on the poisoned air,
    From one with a thorn scarred brow,
"I gave my life for this little soul,
    The soul that I bid for now.

"I give pardon for sin and peace within—
A gem wreathed cross and crown;
Love for hate, and strength to the end,
My smile for the cold world's frown.

"A glorified form and unknown joys,
Eternal life and the victor's song;
Heaven shall ring with anthems of praise,
Sung by the blood washed throng"

The Lord Jesus Christ shall have my dove,
Here, take and make it thine own;
Bought with a price God only can pay,
Made heir to a crown and a throne.

A Woman's Protest.

"We are all more or less religious."—*Globe.*

ALL more or less religious,
Why, even the devils are so,
For they fear God and tremble—
The men deal blow upon blow
On the holy truths of the bible.
I tell you, even to-day,
The Book and God you would suppress,
If some mortals had their way.

Annihilate God! What then?
What if you quench the sun
Till only a blackened coal is left,
   And the day is just begun?
O puny mites that crawl the earth,
   As ants creep over the hill,
Who breathe one moment, die the next,
   Yet prate of their mighty will!

Evolved! From what, I pray you tell?
   And how did the first atom grow?
Wisdom, speak up to a waiting world—
   The race is eager to know.
So much of muscle and brain,
   So much of a finer power
Goes into man, and yet some say
   He's an insect of the hour.

I am only a little woman,
   Yet have just a word to say;
A word for mothers of boys and girls,
   For mothers who love to pray.
I have sent two cherished children
   Into the school on high;
There the Bible is never turned out—
   'T is the text book of the sky.

"A *little* Bible is very good—
  Too much, dyspepsia will give."
Is this your plea, O worthy *Globe?*
  Your logic is like a sieve.
Show me the man who ever died
  Of too much Bible diet;
Latimer, Ridley, do you say?
  Why, that won't keep me quiet.

'T was only the Bible haters
  That put these men to the flame;
Out of this chrism, their souls broke prison,
  And theirs is the martyr's flame.
Have I said my say? No, brother, no—
  The poet is never done;
The woman's heart broke at the wheel,
  And my song for once is sung.

Looking Out.

LOOKING out from the windows of heaven,
  Two little faces I see,
Patiently watching for mamma to come;
  "My darlings, I'm hasting to thee."

It is only waiting a bit, my dears,
   Till the Lord makes ready my place;
Then, like an arrow shot out from the bow,
   I'll gladden each baby face.

Little arms will be clasping my neck,
   Kisses and kisses I'll rain;
The Lord will stand by, and smile to see
   That I am happy again.

So my sweetlings must worship and wait,
   While mamma will serve below;
When at last we meet, our souls will be
   Whiter than whitest of snow.

You must beckon for papa to come,
   Keep waving and waving each hand,
So when we come home we may not miss
   One out of the household band.

When four little white hands are waving
   Their message, "Come up to the sky,"
And Jesus so sweetly is calling,
   I am sure dear papa will try.

To One Who Asked for a Song.

HOW can I sing you a song,
    When the song has gone out of my heart?
How *can* I make sunshine for other homes,
    When I never have learned the art?
The song of the bird is born,
    In its tuneful throat it lies,
Till nature touches the wonderful thing,
    And it soars with a glad surprise ;
Ripple and quaver and trill—
    'T is a tune all unset to words ;
Your heart is stirred with a gladsome thrill,
    And this is the way with the birds.

And *this* is the way with my soul—
    It will fly to the living spring,
To drink the waters, so cool, so sweet,
    Then the song in my heart will ring.
When an arrow flies from the bow,
    It is sure to hit some mark ;
Out into the sunshine fly, little song,
    Though the singer sits in the dark ;
Sparkle and gladden and glow—
    Your wonderful message is love—
Away on your mission I bid you go,
    We will meet in the land above

A marvelous tale is told—
   How the wounded swan, ere she dies,
Breathes the only melody of her life ;
   So the broken in spirit thus cries,
Sending forth a subtle perfume,
   Much finer than mignonette ;
Crushed things are oft times sweeter far,
   We shrink from the process, and yet
Pain's pleasure, sorrow and care,
   Are burning the dross away ;
The pitiful Father will help us bear,
   And teach us to sing hope's lay.

We will turn the cloud, and ever turn,
   For the lining of silver and gold ;
Rare, sweet odors are stealing forth,
   As we fling to the breeze each fold.
There are pity and infinite love,
   A trust that is anchored in heaven,
Wings for a song, and oil for our wound,
   If we search are sure to be given.
Then upward, yet upward, we soar,
   And still as we fly will sing,
'Our nest is built in the clefted rock—
   When the storms roar loudest we'll cling.''

After Christmas.

GOLDEN Christmas bells have stopped their merry ringing,
But up in heaven still, the angels keep on singing;
What a gladsome, merry chime was the bells' sweet midnight song,
With the voices of the angels ringing out, both full and strong.

O how that music swells, like a chime of silver bells,
It beats along the air and the blessed story tells,
Of the babe that found a rest on sweet Mary's snowy breast,
And found the way to heaven from Calvary's rocky crest.

Come help the seraphs sing, till heaven's arches ring,
And peace her glorious banner over all the earth shall fling;
The earth is full of sorrow, so full of want and woe,
But all the climbers upward from Calvary must go.

And once a year, dear friends, we may hope to catch the song,
The spicy gales of heaven are sure to bear along;

Each one of us have crosses, and we faint upon the way,
But the Father he remembers that we are only clay.

O I love to think and ponder on the Motherhood of God,
That He loves to give us kisses, and hates to use the rod;
Rather His chastisements than any earthly crown—
I'm certain were one given, I'd quickly throw it down,

And hunt my thorn wreathed cross, having learned to bear its sting,
And carrying the burden, would have a song to sing.
I am so near my journey's end, the glory shimmers through;
The clouds are breaking in the sky, I catch a glimpse of blue.
So standing on the border land, I raise the victor's shout,
The Christmas bells have rung in peace, and weary souls rung out.

A Little Sermon.

MY brothers, I'll preach you a little
    Wee bit of a sermon, this morn,
Into which I will put the flowers,
    And leave out every thorn.
"Love" is my wonderful topic,
    The shortest divine ever took—
You will find it occurring quite often,
    If you glance within an old book.

Love is the sunlight of heaven,
    God's mighty evangel to men;
It outranks the poet and prophet,
    And conquers the sword and the pen.
Love melts all the frosts of the winter,
    And tempers the summer time heat;
Love ever is bearing our burdens,
    And bringing us low at the feet

Of the Lover that came down from heaven
    To win and to woo mankind;
Love comforts the worn and the weary,
    And opens the eyes of the blind.

What care I for fine spun doctrines,
    With all of the love left out,
While people are starving for gospel,
    And some are beginning to doubt.

I would gladly hold up my Master,
    With His nail marked hands and His feet;
Methinks your hearts would be melted,
    At witnessing love so complete.
Put Christ into all your smiling,
    And into your living as well;
Then the world will be conquered for Jesus,
    And my sermon on love will tell.

Woman.

POETS may dream and women may work,
    Wild bees by the wayside keep humming;
The roses may bud and roses may blow,
    For the good time surely is coming.

I stand in the rift of the present, and feel
    Sweet winds, that are cooling my fever;
With a smile on my lips I am ready to kneel,
    Ere I enter the golden forever.

Our pain and desire are the blossoms I see,
  Not the wonderful fruits they are bearing;
You are toilers to-day—then dig 'round the tree—
  The reaping depends on your daring.

So whether the pitiful rains shall fall,
  Or the sunbeams still keep shining,
Let us never be driven back to the wall,
  Or yield to the demon of whining.

The Call.

'TWAS eighteen hundred years ago,
  The wondrous call was given,
To bearded men in fisher's coats,
  The call from earth to heaven.
They left their boats on Galilee,
  The blue wave's rythmic flowing,
And straight began to sow the seed,
  To-day we see it growing.

The roots are spreading far and wide,
  Sweet winds catch up the story,
And everywhere it goes 'twill give
  An added touch of glory.

'Twas " Peace on earth, Good will to men,"
   The angel bands were singing;
Mankind has caught the heavenly strain,
   O, do n't you hear it ringing.

The bells are swaying to and fro,
   Come, heed the silver pealing,
And worship in God's courts to-day,
   For he will give you healing.
Ah! we are sick of sin and strife,
   While many are so weary,
The hope of gaining freer life,
   Will make *this* life less dreary.

Each little seed that falls to earth
   Is sure of future growing,
And every seed will bear its fruit,
   If God controls the sowing.
One trouble is, we judge the Christ,
   By those who often stumble;
I fancy should we look aloft,
   'Twould make us all more humble.

Some sit by rush-lights, some by stars,
   Some sit beside the fountain,
Whence everlasting light flows down,
   From Zion's holy mountain.

SONGS OF HOPE.

What does the world most need to-day?
　A call to higher living;
A call to love each other more,
　Forgetting and forgiving.

The Bow in the Cloud.

A LOW black cloud comes out of the west;
　The frightened birds fly home to the nest;
The wind gives forth her wailing sound,
While grasses are beaten along the ground.

The arms of the trees are tossing high,
The lightning shaft is cutting the sky;
Down pours the rain on mountain and plain;
But the sun is sure to shine again.

Then you will see God's promise to man—
The rainbow arch in a single span;
It hangs in the air, with colors so rare
You fancy the saints may be walking there.

Our nation is under a cloud,
　Thick darkness is over the land,
I see not the way, but simply cling
　In trust to the dear Father's hand.

When a child is afraid of the dark,
   So much the closer 't will cling;
When a storm is abroad, the mother bird
   Hides the brood close under her wing.
This tempest will sweep to its rest,

   The rainbow will shine in the sky,
Out of our tears and the smiling of God
   Will be painted each glorious dye.
How oft clouds of grief will arise.
   And the pitiless rain will fall,
But every promise of God holds fast,
   He never is deaf to our call.
If the child thinks a stone is its bread,
   Will the mother give that for its cry?
Some plan and purpose too broad for our thought,
   Was the reason why Garfield must die.

"Fear not, little flock, I am here,
   The waters shall not overflow,
Down into the flood so angry and black,
   Along with my children I go;
Look up to my bow in the cloud—
   It arches above the dark grave,
Its colors divine, it cheers one like wine,
   And tints with a glory each wave;

For I will come back and bring in my train
  Your dead made alive by my power;
Then, child, bear the burden and lean on me hard,
  While waiting for me and my hour."

In every cloud of sorrow and sin,
  Christ is set as the rainbow for you;
O, grief stricken souls, look up to the sky,
  His word is both steadfast and true.
While bells of the midnight were tolling for us,
  And Death was undoing the door,
The Master's call was ringing for him,
  And angels came down to the shore
With welcoming songs; the leash of pain,
  So fretted, had broken at last;
Freed spirit that soars beyond the skies,
  Thy woes are all overpast.
We say good night, but very soon
  It will be, "Good morning, friend;"
The sun has risen, again 'tis light,
  And our joy shall never end.
Rainbow of promise, shine on my way,
  Stretch onward from cross unto crown;
Life's restless fever is over soon,
  And we lay our burdens down.

Summer has Come.

QUEEN Summer has come, the blue birds sing,
    Already the roses begin to blow,
Up in the trees the orioles swing,
Out to the breeze the wild flowers fling
    Their dainty robes wove under the snow.

What is the message they bring us to-day,
    For hearts grown heavy with pain and care?
This, the sweet word blown over the way:
"Rejoice in the Lord, and always pray,
    Though your hearts may be heavy and sair.

The day is sure to follow the night,
    The sun will shine again after the storm,
The buried blooms rise up to the light,
Though earth is cold the heavens are bright,
    Our Father above has kept them warm."

Winter came down to his native land,
    Away to the south the birdies flew;
Summer has broken the icy wand,
Uncrowned the king and loosed his hand;
    Now she pipes for her carnival crew.

Whirring wings are athrob in the air,
  The flowers though dead, are alive again,
I hail thee, prophecy, sweet and rare,
Gladly I climb up a golden stair,
  While mounting I catch a glad refrain :

"Sweet things may go—even life may go—
  They wait for you over the river,
For Time sweeps on with a strong, swift flow,
And this one thing you may surely know,
  God holdeth your treasures forever."

Winter is certainly followed by Spring,
  And Spring by the summer time glory ;
I have found my rock and learned to cling,
Let the song in my heart full loudly ring,
  That I learned in the old, old story,

Silver Wedding Song.

HARK to the joyful, jubilant peal,
  The marriage bells are ringing.
We halt before a beautiful gate,
With gifts and blessings here we wait,
Swing wide the way, O, Priestess Fate,
  And see what we are bringing.

To-night I bring a silver thought,
   And braid it with a posy;
For all the silver bells should ring,
And all the white robed angels sing,
While heaven and earth make haste to fling
   Out banners white and rosy.

To-night we halt upon the way,
   And all our lips are smiling;
The bridal rose is fragrant still;
Fill up the golden beaker, fill,
And let your cheers ring with a will—
   Time yields to our beguiling.

To-night we lay our burdens down,
   And all the fret of passion;
Upon the cord of passing years,
Old Time has strung some hopes, some fears,
Perhaps a dash of rainbowed tears,
   For that is old Time's fashion.

To-night we look adown the road,
   Tired with our lengthened climbing;
A silver moon is in the sky,
One shining cloud is floating by,
Hark! Don't you hear a silver cry,
   Now sweetly, softly chiming?

That voice once graced a wedding feast,
   In ancient Galilee;
O, thorn crowned One, come help to twine
White lillies for this festal time,
Come, change our water into wine,
   That we may drink to Thee.

And when thy marriage supper comes,
   May we sit down with singing;
Up there where full banked rivers run,
Where God Himself is shield and sun,
Our toils and cares will then be done,
   While heaven with joy is ringing.

The blossoms of to-night will fade,
   Not those that blow in glory;
Here every rose will have its sting,
Birds often fly with wounded wing,
Some dross unto the silver cling,
   The sequel of earth's story.

O, wedding bells, sweet wedding bells,
Our pulses throb, our full heart swells;
The tear comes welling to our eye,
And yet we feel this joy go by;
But ere 't is gone braid up a prayer,
To crown this newly wedded pair;

MISCELLANEOUS.

We wish your life may never end,
We wish the Lord may be your friend,
We wish—all, let the curtain fall,
Good night, dear friends and brothers all.

Red Clover.

I HAVE been to the blossoming fields to-day,
　　Have caught the scent of the new mown hay,
Have walked knee deep in the clover bloom,
Brought home the red heads to garnish my room;

And now I will sit and tell you over
The graces one finds in pretty red clover,
When dew is upon it like silvery mist,
When sweet winds of morning have airily kissed;

When the God of the sun has wooed it again,
The lark has enthralled with his jubiland strain,
The clover will swing back and forth on her stem,
Entrancing the birds, bees, babies and men.

'Tis a fairylike dance, the butterflies come
To flash their gay wings in the gold of the sun;

The lute of the wind keeps sounding her tune
In the musical way she learned of Miss June.

You almost might think the world had gone mad,
All things are appearing so merry, so glad ;
Nature seems bound by some magical spell—
The clover is only the honey bee's well.

His bronze wings are flashing above each pink cup,
And buckets of honey he soon will draw up,
The while he will drowsily, sleepily hum,
"I love you, sweet clover, and so have I come."

In her tangles red robin has hidden his nest—
The stain of the clover lies thick on his breast;
And there in the nest are blue speckled eggs,
That will turn to beaks and thin yellow legs ;

Will turn to swift wings and bear them along,
When first they essay their glad robin song.
Clover is sweet when it grows by the door,
Sweet by the roadside—'t is sweet evermore :

Sweet in the valley, and sweet on the hill,
The winds of its sweetness have drunken their fill :
My thought is so weak, I cannot tell over
One half of the sweetness that lies in red clover.

'Tis sweet while it lives, and sweet when it dies,
Its fragrance, like incense, steals up to the skies;
Ah! life, you have learned a rare lesson to-day
From the red blooming field just over the way.

Answer to the Nation's Prayer.

WHEN the message flashed over the wires,
   Like a breath from the furnace below,
The national heart was stung to the quick,
   Its beating was heavy and slow.
We thought of the white haired mother then,
   And grieved for the poor stricken wife,
We thought of the children left fatherless,
   And we thought of the nation's life.

The ruffian that dared to strike at him,
   Has wounded us all as well;
The ball that sped on the errand of death,
   Hath worked with a magical spell.
The North and the South, the East and the West,
   Are lavish with prayers and with tears,
This wonderful touch of nature's wand
   Has bridged the wide chasm of years.

We besieged high heaven's pearly walls,
    And we stormed it with our cries;
Over the battlements strong and fair,
    God handed us sweet replies.
We bowed us low down to the dust,
    Lest our chief should go higher still,
We strained at the cable of trust,
    And plead with the infinite will.

The purpose seems dark to our eyes,
    But the poem we read very plain;
We asked a life at the Father's hand,
    And he gave it to us again.
O, life, I will lay thee down,
    Close, close to the Savior's feet;
The answered prayer I will weave in my crown,
    And rejoice in the perfume so sweet.

Into the wine press of the Lord,
    The clusters of grapes were thrown,
This vintage gave to us blood red wine,
    Yet love's white lily has blown,
While over it all God sits and smiles,
    When we pull the latch string of prayer;
We move the One that moveth the world;
    On Him we will cast all our care.

Christ's Transfiguration.

THE spring had come to Palestine, and crowned each hill with flowers,
Blue Galilee laughed out with glee between the summer showers;
While up Mount Hermon's rocky slope four men began to climb—
Three, earthy as the rock itself, while One was all divine.

The birds were singing out their prayers, bright waters broke in foam,
The blue sky stretched above their heads as if 't were heaven's dome;
Ah, heav'n was near to earth that day, and broke the barrier through,
Two came adown some whitened way—the marvel quickly grew.

Transfigured Christ! I dare not try to paint the awful scene,
When so much glory from on high grew like some shining dream;

And one stood there, where ghastly death had never
set his seal,
With Moses, used to mountain tops, and used 'fore
God to kneel.

Ah, soul, I feel thee throb and leap ; at last the trump
shall sound,
To rouse the sleeping nations up—the nations under
ground ;
Yes, then the living shall be changed, all glorious to
the eye,
And rise along some splendid way to meet Christ in
the sky.

The glory hid within the Lord shone out upon that
morn,
The glory hid within myself is waiting to be born ;
All this, and heav'n beside, my friend ; do you wonder
that I cry,
"Break quickly, cloudy heavens, break, and let our
King pass by."

A Mamma to Keep.

A BRIGHT summer morning and all was still,
But the song of a bird just over the hill,
When swiftly there came to my ears a cry,
That God let down from the summer blue sky;
This pitiful call was, "A mamma to keep,"
And what could I do but sit there and weep.

Ah, mothers, whose babies have lain on your breast,
Can you take a wild birdie into the nest?
The poor empty nest that has grown so cold,
Since the clinging hands have unloosened their hold;
Other eyes may be blue and curls look like gold,
Yet we cling to the lambs in the upper fold.

We sit on the edge of our nest, and we wait
The swinging ajar of some pearly gate,
That will let our Lord and the children come through,
Then at last our world will be made over new;
But while we wait and silently weep,
There are birdies that want "a mother to keep."

Babes cannot keep mothers, nor mothers keep sons,
Our souls often die with our dear little ones;
It is worse to have a dead heart in the breast,

Than even to sit in an empty nest;
But still I know well that God is my friend,
He giveth and loveth me, e'en to the end.

But what shall we do with the motherless ones—
Shall we take to us daughters in room of our sons?
And what do we owe to the children that weep,
Who plaintively call for "a mamma to keep?"
Christ leads us, perhaps, by a child's little hand,
Until we cross over to heaven's fair land.

Jesus and the Woman.

TIS a beautiful story, and I'll tell it over,
   It is rarer than diamonds and sweeter than clover,
Its fragrance has drifted along down the ages,
With a charm for the lowly and grace for the sages.

Let me paint you the scene this beautiful morning,
The smile of a God is my canvas adorning,
   And out of it grows the rare, wonderful story,
   That once lighted the hills of Judea with glory.

It was only a woman, her black hair unbanded,
They had hunted her down—with shame she was
    branded;
    She stood with bowed head and clasped hands in
        her sorrow,
Not hoping to see the glad sunshine to-morrow.

There were men with stern brows and lips void of pity,
Standing ready to stone this poor waif of the city;
    She had broken the law, and frail man, unforgiving,
    Would hurl her away, name and place from the
        living.

One with presence divine among them was standing,
In form and in feature alike was commanding;
    His voice, sweet and calm, through the tumult was
        stealing,
    Swift winged were his words, bringing wisdom and
        healing.

"Let him cast the first stone who has ne'er wronged
    a brother,
For only the stainless should judge one another."
    Jesus stooped to the ground and wrote with His
        finger—
    Guilty men, self accused, not long did they linger.

"Has no man accused thee?" She answered, "No,
  Master,"
While still she was speaking, her poor heart beat faster;
  "Then neither do I." She went out forgiven,
Her life was reprieved, one chance more for heaven.

CHILDS DEPARTMENT.

Little Boy Blue.

OH, little boy true, with breeches of blue,
  How much do you love me to-day?
"A bushel and peck, with my arms 'round your neck;
  And now let me run out to play."

What makes you so sweet from your head to your feet?
  "Sugar candy, I guess, does n't you?"
And what makes you cry—can you tell me why?
  "Old *naughty* man; now is you through?"

Not yet little dear; this tiny pink ear—
    What can it be good for? Just think.
"To hear birdies sing, and most everything—
    I'm firsty, please get me a dink."

A cherry red mouth, the wind from the south
    Is not sweeter than this dewy lip;
Let's play I'm a bee, and happen to see
    A posy; I'm after a sip.

"My mouf's good to kiss, but mamma, I wiss
    That you wouldn't bodder me so."
Your two little eyes, that are blue as the skies,
    Just tell where you got them, then go.

God cut from the sky a bit for my eye;
    It left a round hole in the floor,
Through the crack at night comes a star for light—
    Please mamma, don't ask any more."

To Gracie's Picture.

OH fathomless eyes, looking up to the skies,
    What mysteries do you behold?
In some favoring gale, will your soul set sail,
    Leaving us but the empty fold?

But let me tell your graces o'er,
Sweet Grace, that lit upon our shore
    One sunny spring time day;
Your ways are quaint, your words are wise,
I know you learned them in the skies.
    When angels were at play.

But then they left an open gate
Through which you flew so swift, so straight
    Into my throbbing breast;
I clipped your wings and held you fast
Until the hunt was overpast,
    My heart is now your nest.

This fragrant hair my fingers twine,
Like curling tendrils of the vine,
    Breathes spices at my touch;
Upon your brow God set his seal,
I dare not tell you what I feel,
    And dare not love too much.

If He should call you back some day,
I'd quickly find the upward way
   And woo you home again.
But God is love—of that I'm sure,
Long as the ages shall endure
   He will not break love's chain.

Oh, mouth that angels loved to kiss,
I wonder if they ever miss
   My darling from their throng?
Heaven had grown so full, you see,
They gave this girlie up to me,
   And turned my life to song.

Christmas Carol.

DEAR children, I come with my carol to-night.
   For the glad Christmas bells are a ringing;
The heavens are full and the earth overflows
   With wonderful, wonderful singing.
So, take up the measure and send it along,
   Let us tell the fair angels our story,
How the Savior came down, and how we shall go
   To live with him yet in his glory.

A fair, smiling baby, he lay on the breast
  Of Mary, his fond, happy mother;
Such a wonderful lullaby she sang to him,
  The world never heard such another.
Where did she learn it, my questioning babes?
  She heard what the angels were singing,
As they halted midway 'twixt the heavens and earth,
  When the heavens and earth were both ringing.

What was the song, darlings? Why I'll tell it over:
  It was peace and good will to the people,
The bells caught it up and are telling it still,
  Its echoes are filling each steeple,
This hymn, once begun on the plains of Judea,
  Has become the sweet march of the ages,
'T is lisped by the baby when falling asleep,
  'T is chanted in death by the sages.

'T will be sung in the sunshiny meadows of heaven,
  Where the throng that no mortal can number
Are gathered with harps and with crowns on their heads;
  Will we join in that music, I wonder?
What a passion of song to break at his feet,
  The baby of Bethlehem's story;
The heavens shall echo the melody sweet,
  And the earth shall be filled with his glory.

Staining of the Leaves.

ONE breezy, golden tipped autumn day,
    When odors of spices were out at play,
I gathered a troop, and led the way
Over the hills, with spirits so gay.

Jack Frost had been out for many a night,
The woods were ablaze with rainbow light;
I stood entranced with the gorgeous sight,
Evoked by the wand of the ice born wight.

I sat on a log while each girl and boy,
Their hearts o'erflowing with mirth and joy,
Flitted about in the sweet employ
Of gathering what the frost would destroy.

The golden buds of the bittersweet
They brought, and heaped around my feet;
The scarlet leaves flew down to greet
The hearts, that flew up with a happy beat.

Russet and bronze were the gathered leaves,
Crimson and yellow are autumn's sheaves;
'T is a royal chaplet that Nature weaves
For the dying year, o'er which she grieves.

Wild woods scents sprang under our tread,
The sun shone down from over our head,
And ere we knew it the day had sped—
This beautiful day that God had led.

Yet before we took our homeward way,
I gathered the children, weary with play,
And told them a story to round the day,
I learned from a fairy over the way :

> When the royal word went out,
>   Every fairy gave a shout,
> And the staining of the leaves
>   We quickly went about.
>
> Each one stole a pot of dye,
>   From the rainbow in the sky,
> And we promised her to pay,
>   If we could, by and by.
>
> Up and down the trees we climbed,
>   Oh, we had a merry time!
> As we daubed the red and yellow—
>   Here a dot and there a line.
>
> Fairies hung on every twig—
>   Fairies little, fairies big ;
> Some were laughing, some were talking—
>   Lazy fairies danced a jig.

The wind was drunk with pleasure,
  The sun filled up earth's measure
With pale, autumnal gold,
  Nor missed it from her treasure.

This the way the leaves were stained,
  Hazy purple and azure veined
The air, earth, sea and sky,
  While over all God reigned.

The fairies I sing of when all is done,
Are only the fairies of frost and sun,
So joy and grief have life webs spun,
For souls to wear when heaven is won.

It is now a jet, and now a pearl,
The shuttle flies with a ceaseless whirl
For every glad hearted boy and girl,
Till the loom is stopped, and life's flag furled.

Going Fishing.

"I'M going fishing, mamma, dear,
　　On this very afternoon,
For papa said I might, you know—
　　I am crazy as a loon.
Now I must run and hunt some bait,
　　And fix my hook and line ;
If I should catch an *awful* fish,
　　I should need a stronger twine."

"My darling, don't you hurry so—
　　I have a tale to tell ;
There's time enough to get your bait,
　　If you wait a little spell.
They had killed our blessed Jesus,
　　And put Him in the grave ;
Some hearts were sad—they thought this man,
　　Lost Israel's race would save.

"Peter uprose, so bold in speech,
　　But sick at heart was he :
'I go afishing ;' others said,
　　'We go along with thee.'
So seven men went straightway out
　　On Galilee's blue sea ;

They toiled all night and nothing caught,
    Then morn came o'er the lea.

"Toiled all night till the moon went down,
    And now at the break of day,
They drew their empty nets again,
    Up through the waters gray.
'Cast in your nets on the other side,'
    A cry rang out from land;
The loving John quick knew the voice—
    He looked across the sand,

"And cried, 'It is our risen Lord;
    He has come and calls for me.'
Then Simon girt his fisher's coat,
    And straight plunged in the sea;
A craven once, but now the first
    To reach the white sea sand;
The others came in a little boat,
    In a little boat to land.

"A fire of coals they quickly saw—
    Ah! 't was a gladsome sight,
For they were tired, and wet, and cold,
    With toiling all the night.
The Savior's gentle, loving voice
    Said, 'Children, dine with me;

And all this happened long ago,
  By stormy Galilee.

"They dined, and then the Master turned;
  'O Simon, lov'st thou me?'
He asked him once, he asked him thrice,
  'Simon, dost thou love me?
Then feed my sheep and feed my lambs,
  Until I come once more;'
And then they slowly walked away,
  From Galilee's bleak shore.

"And all adown the hoary years,
  Cometh this pleading cry:
'Lovest thou me? lovest thou me?
  For thee I once did die.'
I would, my son, that thou couldst say,
  As fiery Peter said,
'Lord, thou dost know that I love thee—
  I'll follow where I'm led.'"

Mother Goose Revised.

"SING a song o' sixpence,"
　　Sitting in the sun,
All the babies round me,
　　Waiting for the fun;
Clap your hands in motion,
　　Swing them up and down,
While I sing a ditty,
　　Of what they do in town.

" A pocket full of rye,"
　　But not a bit for you ;
Rye would make you tipsy,
　　And that would never do.
" Four and twenty blackbirds,
　　Baked into a pie,"
Is better for my babies
　　Than whisky made of rye.

" Four and twenty blackbirds "
　　Sell it on the street ;
It will muddle babies' heads,
　　And tangle babies' feet.

The temperance folks are baking
   For them a little pie,
To make them quit the selling
   Their pocket full of rye.

"When the pie is opened,
   The birds will 'gin to sing,"
And every snowy angel
   Will wave a snowy wing.
Let us be up and doing,
   And help to roll along,
The pie that we are baking,
   We want to hear the song.

"Won't it be a dainty dish
   To set before our King?"
Methinks he will begin to smile,
   When the birds begin to sing.
Who is the King of Glory,
   That wants to hear the song?
'T is Jesus, up in heaven—
   Don't keep Him waiting long.

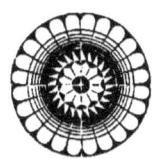

The Kitten Story.

ONE little girlie bending there,
   Her eyes are full of mother care;
Two little kittens tucked in bed,
Each with a nightcap on his head.
Three little fingers rocked the crib—
Now, kitties, do as you are bid;
Four little eyes go right to sleep—
Don't you even dare to peep.

One little tongue wags along,
Singing kittie's sleepy song;
Two little kittens jump and run,
With their night caps into the sun.
Three little squeals and away she goes—
The kittens hide beneath the rose;
Four bright eyes that just peep out—
Kitties know what they're about.

One little hand goes swiftly in,
Two little kittens scratch the skin;
Pretty soon they all three go
In to mamma, with their woe.
Both the kittens lash their tails,
While the tiny maiden wails;
Four light taps on each kit's ear,
Then the sky begins to clear.

Whisky Punch.

WHISKY Punch was a very bad boy,
Who made more trouble than he gave joy,
His mother shed a river of tears,
Her heart was always convulsed with fears;
"O, Whisky Punch, what shall I do?
I wish that I were rid of you."
"But, mother, you can't, I'm here, you see,
You had better make the best of me."

Whisky Punch had a cousin, my dear,
He went by the name of Lager Beer,
And every man who was his friend,
Purchased a nose bright red at the end.
So, if you join the whisky clan,
This is the badge to wear, my man,
They furnish lodgings free to you,
You lie in the gutter when you get through.

Lie in the gutter along with the pigs,
And pay for it all with whisky swigs,
The mother resolved one autumn day,
To send her Whisky Punch away,

And well she knew that in his rear,
Would quickly follow Lager Beer;
She set on his brow the mark of Cain,
And said : " Don't you ever come back again."

But the boys declared, " We will not go,
If you try that game the blood will flow;
Here we are and we mean to stay,
You had better let us alone, I say."
" Let you alone, that's what you say?
And what I intend to after this day."
The mother arose in might and power,
And thrust them out within the hour;

Then locked the door with gleaming eye,
Those naughty boys thought to defy
My righteous law—well, let them go,
Nobody wants them, that I know.
Pephaps some day, they'll gladly come
Back to their mother and their home.
" Ah, boys, I'll gladly let you in,
If you leave outside that hideous sin."

CHILDS DEPARTMENT.

Going a Maying.

COME children from a thousand folds,
   And let us go a Maying;
Come, locks of brown and locks of gold,
   The summer winds are playing;
I am so glad, my two old feet
   Can hardly keep from dancing:
So, regiment of babies, march—
   I want to see you prancing.

Yes, we will go right straight afield,
   And fight the queerest battle,
We will not fire a single gun,
   Nor heed the drummer's rattle.
The bugle of the honey-bee,
   I hear it shrilly blowing,
And all the merry, mad-cap brooks
   Laugh out, but still keep going.

We'll slaughter all the buttercups—
   Those gaudy golden fellows,
Spring flowers should bloom in white and blue,
   And not in vulgar yellows;

The dainty wind-flowers for your spoil—
    Blue violets so cunning—
They hide among the meadow grass
    And whisper, "Summer's coming!"

Gnarled apple trees, thick-set with bees,
    Transfigured by the glory
That breaks in creamy pink and white,
    You mind us of the story
How Mother Eve from Eden fell,
    Won by your subtle charming,
While father Adam comfort gained
    By going straight to farming.

My soldiers dear, oh, don't you hear
    The birdies at their revel?
Blue-birds and robins, what a noise—
    Their heads are hardly level!
Now let us march right home again,
    Our arms with treasures laden,
But ere we part, I would enlist
    For Christ each lad and maiden.

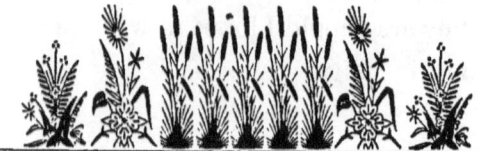

Nellie's Chatter.

MAMMA, look out! I dess old Movver Doose
   Is emty'n her nice fedder bed,
How bu'ful it looks jist hoppin' along,
   I love the white snow, Nellie said.

"Know where it tums from? right down from Dod,
   The angels are sweepin' the floor;
If it didn't tum down quite so fast, you know,
   I could see right into the door.

"The angels are wearin' white frocks like me,
   I dess I'm a bright angel too;
I would like to do and live up in heaven,
   But, movver, I tould n't leave you.

"You want me to hug and tiss when you're tired;
   Then, mamma, I have n't dot wings,
I'll be just as dood as ever I tan,
   You'll smile when your little dirl sings.

"Dod has dot such a lot of angels you see,
   And mamma have only dot one;
So, if the angels should want me up dere,
   I'd say I tant *possibly* tum.

"Scuse me, dear angel, but mamma would cry,
    If I left her alone you see,
Ev'ry night I tuddle up close to her side,
    And say all my prayers at her knee.

Red Breast Robin.

BEFORE the flowers begin to blow,
    Robin begins to sing;
Before the trees have dressed themselves,
    He heralds in the spring.
What is he saying, baby dear?
Open your mouth and you will hear;
You open wide those blue, blue eyes,
And lift them up to the bluer skies.

"God is talking to me and you."
Babies words are quaint but true,
Hear him ripple, quaver and trill,
    Spilling his melody into the air,
Singing his praise beyond the hill—
    Our darlings are sweetly sleeping there.
Baby was right, 't was the voice of God—
Our loved ones sleep beneath the sod,
They'll come again some joyous spring,
And I with robin red breast will sing.

Two Johnnies.

ONE Johnny lived in the country,
 And one Johnny lived in town,
One had eyes, blue as the skies,
 And the other had eyes of brown.

Country John was up with the sun,
 Away to the meadow went he,
Brown, bare feet, and a whistle so sweet,
 While his steps were swinging and free.

A torn straw hat on a curly head;
 So Johnny went trudging along,
Brushed from the grass, dew drops as he passed,
 And he mimicked the blue bird's song.

Wild roses abloom in the hedges,
 Sir squirrel frisks over the way,
The boy was in tune, with a rolicking June,
 Oh, to bring up the cows was play.

Johnny, who lives in the city,
 Got out of his bed at eight,
Cross as a bear, and he did n't care,
 When mamma said, "You are late."

Breakfast must down in a hurry,
 And the laddie went off to school,

Tired body and brain, with constant strain,
    Lest Johnny might turn out a fool.
Better a boy on a horse's back,
    That lashed to the page of a book;
Out from the street, lead the dear feet,
    At Nature's fair page bid them look.
Build muscle first and then the brain,
    If you want the boys to be men,
To take high place, in life's swift race,
    Either with plow or with pen.

Snow Flake.

BABY is at the window,
    Watching the snow come down,
Spreading a mantle of whiteness
    Over the country and town
"Where does it come from, mamma?
    I really would like to know."
God sends it to us, my darling,
    And we call it beautiful snow."
"God, I'm looking up at you,
    Do you see my two little eyes?"
I think that he sees my treasure
    From his home beyond the skies.

Somebody's Coming.

SANTA CLAUS is coming,
  Oh, don't you hear the news?
Santa Claus is coming,
So I'll pull off my shoes,
For under shoes are stockings,
And stockings hold my feet;
Just now it's my opinion,
They 'll soon hold something sweet.
Boys and girls like candy,
And "Santa" knows that well--
He's coming with his bags full,
And something else to sell;
He may give the girls the dollies,
But boys are fond of drums—
I'm crazy for the racket
I'll make when Santa comes.
Gran'ma will say, "O dearie,
Please don't make such a noise,"
But gran'mammas could never
Feel just like little boys.
I guess my precious mother
Will let me pound away—
She knows it makes boys happy,
To have a *splendid* play.

I don't believe in heaven
    They ever say, "keep still—"
I'd rather stay down here awhile,
    If it is Jesus' will.

I wonder how Saint Santa looks?
    He's just a funny fellow—
He always wears a bear skin coat,
    His beard is awful yellow;

He drives a span of reindeer,
    But I never hear them go—
The curious thing about it is,
    No tracks are in the snow.

They say he comes down chimneys,
    When everyone's asleep;
Hadn't I better lie awake,
    And at him slyly peep?

But mamma says it's naughty,
    For one to try and spy,
And always when her little boy
    Does wrong, mamma will cry.

The very nicest present,
    That ever he did bring,
Was a cunning little baby,
    That made the angels sing.

See here, now, I'm just thinking,
   It seems a little queer,
For stables have no chimneys—
   What did Santa do that year?
Gretchen told me this morning,
   He sometimes brings a rod;
I should'nt wonder, after all,
   If Santa Claus was God.

Little Bare Feet.

OUT of the house and into the sun,
   Two little bare feet swiftly run,
Bonnie blue eyes and yellowish curls,
And this is our Queenie among the girls.
Dimpled white feet skipping along,
Rosy red lips that blossom in song—
Methinks I will cage the song that she sings,
This birdie of ours without any wings.

"Oh, I am so glad the winter is done,
   And I am so glad to be out in the sun;
Buttercups, buttercups, come with your gold,
The winter is dead, and spring's growing old.
Johnny Jump-up, I am glad to see you—
   Did you have a hard time to work your way th

Mr. Robin, I hope that you see my bare feet—
The grass is so cool and the air is so sweet."

To-day and to-morrow the roses may blow,
But, little bare feet, how little we know
What thorns you may find in the pathway you tread ;
Though the thorns are beneath, there is God
   overhead.
So gather the blossoms, my darling, to-day,
December will follow so quickly on May ;
There is never a season but harvests some sweet,
And this you will find, my Little Bare Feet.

The daffy-down-dillies look up to the sky,
And so, little Dimple Cheeks, let's you and I ;
A few weeks ago all the flowers went to bed,
And some little people thought they were dead.
But through the brown earth they now have pricked
   through,
And here is a lesson for me and for you :
Although the dear Jesus may take these bare feet,
To walk or to run on His golden paved street,

They will come back again ; I will list to their tread,
For here is God's promise of life from the dead ;
And though you may walk the rough highway of
   years,

Till your feet are all scarred, your eyes dim with
    tears,
Reach up to the light, keep pressing along,
At last you shall join in the glorified song;
There were thorns for the Savior—you may suffer,
    my sweet,
But Jesus will guide home those little bare feet.

Longing for Spring.

DEAR mother, I'm tired of the Winter,
    And long for the beautiful Spring;
She is wonderful slow in coming,
    And Winter's a hateful old thing.

He's nothing but snow storm and bluster,
    With an icicle for his wand;
The soft footed Spring is coming, to strew
    Dainty posies all over the land.

Then away to the caves of the Northland,
    Old Winter will hurry and run;
He's afraid of the spice winds of Summer,
    And afraid of the blazing hot sun.

He tore from the trees their green laces,
    He put all the flowers in bed,

Then wove a white spread to cover them up,
  To make people believe they were dead.
Down in the brown earth they are hiding,
  The purple, the white and the red;
By and by they'll hop out so happy and bright,
  When Spring tramps along overhead.
The frogs in the pond will be piping,
  Honey bees in their hives then will hum,
Mrs. Robin and Bluebird keep house again—
  So hurry up, Miss Spring, and come.
You see my Spring's work, it is coming,
  There'll be violets and birds' eggs to find;
Such treasures of mosses to gather,
  Downy flocks of chickies to mind.
Good bye to you, Mr. White Winter,
  We are both in a hurry to go;
I must hasten to welcome the spring time,
  And you in the Northland may snow.

Baby.

EYES like two pansies and mouth like a rose.
  And just the funniest bit of a nose;
Hands like a cupid, brow like a God,
Then the sweet darling can wink and can nod.

When he is sleepy he's most sure to cry,
Until the dear mamma is ready to fly;
But she knows so well how to manage the elf,
And tuck him away on sleepy man's shelf.

She puts the brown head close under her wing,
And straightway begins to coo and to sing.
This is the picture of baby you see—
A king in the house—his throne mamma's knee.

Though he keep us awake more than half the night,
We call him our darling, our treasure, delight;
Rock-a-bye baby, my baby so blest,
Now I'll cuddle you down in a soft, little nest.

Sleeping and smiling—was there ever before
Such a wonderful child as flew in at our door?
Yes, one that was cradled on Mary's white breast—
I love you, my pet, but He loves you best.

"Didn't Want to be an Angel."

I DON'T want to be an angel,
    And with the angels stand—
I'd rather be a little boy,
    And play in this white sand;

I'll heap it up and heap it up,
    Until it is so high,
They'll think the tower of Babel
    Is bumping 'gainst the sky.
And then the angels will look out
    And say, "That little boy
Is having such a happy time,
    His heart's brim full of joy.
I shouldn't wonder they would like
    To play in this nice sand,
I think that it is jolly
    To sift it through my hand.

Now, if I was an angel,
    And always dressed in white,
Mamma would never scrub me up
    And say, "He's such a fright."
I tell you it is awful—
    Soap suds gets in my eye,
And then it's pretty certain,
    That I'll begin to cry.

The angels stand on nothing,
    I stand upon my feet,
And when my sleepy time is come,
    My mamma says I'm sweet;

She can beat the angels singing,
　Of that I'm pretty sure,
And when my head is almost broke,
　Her kisses are my cure.
I wonder what the angels do
　When they get tired or hurt ;
I should n't think it would be nice
　To never play in dirt.
I will *never* be an angel,
　Not even if I can ;
I'd rather be a little boy,
　Till I'm a grown up man.

Christmas Bells.

IT comes around just once a year—
　The blessed Christmas chiming—
Just once a year my lips are touched,
　And bloom in Christmas rhyming.
I will sing for all the children,
　Upon this side of glory,
The lyric of the angel band,
　'T is Bethlehem's old story.

Come, gather, gather round me,
　While heaven's bells are pealing,
Adown the solemn midnight sky,
　The melody is stealing.

I see, as in a vision rare,
   The baby in its cradle,
A light that was not born out of earth
   Fills up the lowly stable.

'Tis a King on Mary's bosom,
   Fling out each snowy banner,
For heaven and earth resound to-night,
   As children shout "Hosanna."
Methinks the choirs of heaven stop,
   To hear the sweet voiced singing,
This hymn of Jesus belts the earth,
   'Tis ever ringing, ringing.

Braid up the holly and the green,
   To deck the Infant's cradle,
For Christ came down one Christmas night,
   And glorified a stable,
Yes, He will come again to earth—
   Sweet winds take up the story—
The quivering sky will break her bars,
   To let him out of glory.

www.ingramcontent.com/pod-product-compliance
Lightning Source LLC
Chambersburg PA
CBHW020925230426
43666CB00008B/1575